## GUIDANCE FROM A MASTER

James H. Hoke is one of America's leading therapeutic hypnotists.

In his years of experience, James H. Hoke has perfected a method to allow men and women to achieve dramatically swift and amazingly effective results all by themselves—*without hypnosis*.

Whether you want to get rid of negative factors holding you back, or to fulfill your total promise, it is now within your power if you follow the step-by-step instructions in the most important book that will ever change your life—

# I WOULD IF I COULD AND I CAN

# I Would If I Could And I Can

## JAMES H. HOKE

BERKLEY BOOKS, NEW YORK

This Berkley book contains the complete
text of the original hardcover edition.
It has been completely reset in a typeface
designed for easy reading and was printed
from new film.

I WOULD IF I COULD AND I CAN

A Berkley Book / published by arrangement with
Stein and Day

PRINTING HISTORY
Stein and Day edition published 1980
Berkley edition / October 1982
Third printing / April 1987

ISBN: 0-425-10067-7

A BERKLEY BOOK ® TM 757,375
Berkley Books are published by The Berkley Publishing Group,
200 Madison Avenue, New York, New York 10016.
The name "BERKLEY" and the stylized "B" with design
are trademarks belonging to Berkley Publishing Corporation.
PRINTED IN THE UNITED STATES OF AMERICA

*To Lenore Bechtel,*
*who as my collaborator, confidante, and friend*
*made the publication of this book possible.*

# Contents

# Preface

THIS BOOK APPLIES the remarkable curative techniques of hypnosis to a method that can be used by anyone to change his life. Just as I have personally assisted thousands of people to stop smoking, lose weight, change their jobs, their marriages, the way they look, and even the way they act, I can teach you how to become what you want to be.

As a hypnotist with a clinical practice since 1967, I have served as a consultant to doctors, dentists, mental health clinics, and law enforcement agencies. And I have seen thousands of people helped by my techniques. I help them by attacking how they *feel*, not how they think. Most people already know what their problems are, and they may have even thought out the solution. But they can't change—because they don't have the right emotions and the necessary emotional drive. In fact, their emotions are stopping them.

You need to change these emotions before you can lead a successful life. And you don't need a hypnotist to do it for you. A hypnotic trance is nothing more than a professional way of relaxing and releasing your emotions. I can teach you to do this on your own, in your own home, with the step-by-step method I have perfected for more than thirteen years.

My technique of psychofusion will teach you how to direct your own life, how to fuse the right emotions into your intellectual framework. Psychofusion is a method to bring out your ingrained abilities. It uses only what is already there inside you.

You already possess all that is necessary to change your life. This book will give you the tools to bring your best feelings forth and use them positively.

# PART ONE

# Programming That Made You What You Are

# CHAPTER 1

# Your Accidental Feelings

As A HYPNOTIST I see amazing things happen with people's minds every day. I see production line workers transform themselves into independent businessmen, frumpy housewives become stunning femmes fatales, mediocre athletes excel at their sports, stutterers talk as plainly as you and I.

That's why I know that you—just like everyone else in the world—have untapped capabilities concealed inside of you. I've learned to help people tap those capabilities and scratch the fatalistic belief of "That's just the way I am. I can never change."

They change! Nail biters stop chewing at their fingers, chain smokers throw away their cigarettes, fat people stop stuffing themselves, fearful flyers board a Concorde and cross the Atlantic.

You too can change into the person you'd like

to be. With what I've learned by using hypnosis as a catalyst for self-help, I can teach you self-psych techniques to turn on the best in you and turn off the worst, to change your accidental life to a life you choose on purpose.

You got to be the way you are because of things programmed into the subconscious computer bank that controls the 90 percent of you that's emotional. Your computer beats your heart and breathes for you. It blinks your eyes faster in a sandstorm and pumps your adrenalin faster in an emergency. Your computer causes you to shield your face if somebody throws something at it.

Just as it automatically makes such physical decisions in your best interest, it also makes emotional decisions—some of which keep you chained to your childhood emotional programming.

You don't have to settle for accidental feelings programmed into your subconscious. Because you have every possible human emotion within you, you can retrieve the best to make yourself a better person.

Start by getting rid of the self-defeating feeling of guilt. Stop feeling guilty because you're not perfect. In fact, unless you can eliminate irrational guilts from your subconscious, you will be stifled in your attempt to change.

Once you accept the view that your feelings and attitudes are part of your accidental subconscious programming, why feel guilty about your short-comings? Shortcomings they might be—but you didn't choose them. Because they resulted from your accidental programming, you don't need to take them personally. Don't blame yourself. Take those shortcomings objectively as a product of your subconscious that you choose to change.

Although none of us was born with guilt, we were programmed to it at an early age. Obviously, some guilt feelings are necessary for a civilized society. If a driver didn't feel guilty running a red light, we'd have one traffic accident after another. Such a rational guilt, serving as a conscience that gives us a sense of right and wrong, helps people live harmoniously in our environment. Other, irrational guilts manifest themselves in negative feelings.

We learned to feel guilty as children when our parents punished us for doing things they didn't like. When we feel guilty as adults, we subconsciously want the punishment that will eliminate the guilt and make us feel all right again. If that punishment doesn't come from others, some people supply it for themselves, either by demonstrating self-destructive behavior or allowing guilt feelings to suppress their personal growth. Excessive guilt results in low self-esteem that perpetuates the self-fulfilling prophecy of a loser.

Myra's guilt caused her to damage her face and conceal her body. A 23-year-old natural beauty, Myra habitually scratched and picked at her face all day and all night. Her complexion was badly marred by scratch scabs, and her clothes were tattered, worn, and baggy enough to hide her tiny waistline and trim hips.

Under hypnosis I age-regressed her to the time she first unconsciously began picking at her face. The destructive habit began six years before when her mother's beautiful face was shattered in an auto accident. Until then, people frequently commented about how alike the family's two beauties were in their loveliness. Myra's guilt about still being attractive, while her mother faced years of plastic surgery, caused her to deface herself. Only after reprogramming her subconscious perception of her mother's unfortunate accident was she able to stop punishing herself for her guilt.

Although Myra chose hypnosis to discover the reason for her problem, she could have isolated the reason by herself had she honestly tried. Once she guided her thoughts back to when her face-picking habit started, she certainly could have connected it with the accident that damaged her mother's face. Knowing what prompted her bad habit would be the first step toward eliminating it, along with the guilt that accompanied it.

Guilt keeps people from growing, causing them to punish themselves, looking for the penance their subconscious childhood programming tells them they need.

Ray advanced from a mechanic for recreational vehicles to a salesman, but he had trouble closing sales although he knew recreational vehicles backward and forward. He had taken them apart and put them together for 15 years, and no other company salesman knew the product better than he.

Under hypnosis Ray's subconscious revealed his problem. Ray was accustomed to sweating and getting dirty as he worked with his hands as a mechanic. Although, intellectually, his conscious mind recognized that advancing from a mechanic to a salesman was commendable, emotionally his subconscious mind disagreed, feeling that selling wasn't genuine toil. Because selling didn't require physical exertion and perspiration, his subconscious equated it with laziness. He sub-consciously required himself to abort sales as punishment for his guilt.

Quiet introspection could have led Ray to the same reason for his problem that hypnosis did. In spite of wanting to be a good salesman, he didn't feel good about his job. If he had started analyzing possible reasons for that bad feeling, he would eventually have pinpointed guilt as the only logical reason. Pinpointing the guilt and recognizing it as illogical, he would have been able to change his feeling on his own, just as I did when he was hypnotized.

Ray's particular guilt is very common in our technological society. Because most Americans are programmed with the hard-work ethic, many subconsciously believe physical, dirty work is more ennobling than intellectual work. Many a man feels guilty wearing a business suit, sitting at a desk all day, and making more money than his coal-mining father ever did. The subconscious doesn't sort out the facts: that the man lives in a different era than his father, that his father slaved to give him an opportunity for a better job, that advancing beyond his father's lot should make him proud, not guilty. The subconscious doesn't intellectualize. It only feels.

Obviously, guilt is a waste of time. Why, then, go through life feeling guilty about past acts that can't be changed?

"If I'd known then what I know now, I'd never have done that" is an often-repeated refrain that keeps people dissatisfied with themselves. Such people have their perspectives messed up. If they hadn't done those things, they wouldn't have had the experience to look back on and to help them understand their shortcomings. They wouldn't have had the opportunity to grow. You know now that certain things you did weren't so proper, moral, fair, or respectable because of where you are now. But you are not there in the past when those things you feel guilty about happened. You are here in the present, and you have learned that certain past actions were not admirable. If you hadn't come through the bad times that accompany growing, learning, and maturing, you wouldn't know the difference.

Looking back and judging something in your past as bad should make you feel good. Being capable of making that judgment indicates you've grown. Otherwise you'd be judging your past actions by the same criteria as five years ago, fifteen years ago, or even fifty.

So forget the guilt trip, forget the past, forget the self-recriminations. Begin to treat your subconscious like a companion that deserves special attention. Be friends with it. Don't let it be your enemy because it's programmed with things you don't like that make you dislike yourself.

Treat it like you treat your heart. Basically, you ignore your heart until it gives you trouble. You know it's there in your body, beating to keep you alive, but you take it for granted until something goes wrong. Then you begin to pamper it to keep it working longer and extend your life.

The same should be true of your subconscious. If your accidental programming gave you a positive trip, you're satisfied with the emotions your subconscious chooses for you. In life's flip of the coin, you got heads—and that's great. You can afford to continue ignoring your subconscious mind, just the way you ignore your heart as long as it's beating correctly.

However, if your subconscious gives you trouble—if it makes you apprehensive when you'd like to be secure, if it makes you depressed when you'd like to be happy—don't be satisfied with the negative trip your life's accidents selected for you. You got a bad toss in life's game of chance, but you don't have to settle for the tails that came up.

Start pampering your subconscious. Selectively reject the programming you don't like. Don't personalize your shortcomings, but accept them objectively as part of your package you choose not to keep. Once you reprogram that package with feelings you choose for yourself, the life you want will be within your grasp.

**INSTANT RECALL:** "My life won't be built on useless guilt."

# CHAPTER 2

# Your Childhood Emotional Programming

YOU COME OUT of a warm womb into a brightly lighted, cold place where somebody dangles you upside down and slaps your bottom to make you cry. The new environment doesn't feel very welcoming, so you scream like hell. But then you get some good feelings. A nurse holds you close, getting you warm again, and you get to suck on something pleasurable.

Feelings dominate the first few years of your life. Those feelings—good or bad—are the foundation for the subconscious computer that controls the 90 percent of you that's emotional.

Most people think their intellects control their lives. Wrong!

If intellect controlled our lives, we'd have no fat people in the world. It doesn't take a genius to know that fat is unhealthy. When you huff and puff climbing two flights of stairs, your heart is working overtime. No one has to tell you that. When excess weight prohibits racquetball or tennis or maybe even croquet, you're smart enough to know you're not getting proper exercise to keep your body healthy.

Your intelligence doesn't eat; your emotions eat. You eat because it feels good, not because you're smart or because you're stupid. You can have an IQ of 190 and weigh 290 pounds.

If intellect controlled our lives, would our air be polluted by smokers puffing away at something they know can harm them? Most smokers know they are twenty times more apt to develop lung cancer than non-smokers. They know they're increasing their chances of a heart attack six times. They don't smoke because they think they should or because they want to. They smoke because it feels good. What's more, if they try to quit smoking, it feels bad. They yell at their kids, gripe at their spouses, and weep uncontrollably for no reason at all. Their feelings smoke, not their thinking.

That 10 percent of us that's intellectual just can't cut it by itself. The 90 percent of us that's emotional will be the winner almost every time. If you're going to stop overeating, stop smoking, or stop anything that prevents you from being the person you want to be, you've got to reach the 90 percent of you that's emotional. You've got to get down to your computer, which has been haphazardly programmed to control the way you are. You can't change the computer's output unless you can control the power terminal. If you don't like your life—if it doesn't feel good—you need to change it.

Most of what you are is an accident—physically, intellectually, and emotionally. Physically, you're just living inside the shell that was given to you, unless you're one of the rare one-percenters who's developed your body into a shape you've chosen. Intellectually you've learned only what you've been exposed to, and only a small slice of that was on purpose—like most other aspects of your life. If you're satisfied with your physical and intellectual self, you got a lucky toss of the coin. Congratulations! If you're not satisfied, join the crowd. You're not the only one who got short-changed.

Emotionally you've been programmed by what was available to you. If you're a crybaby, it's not because you chose that attention-getting route. If you can take the hard knocks and come out smiling, it's because of a fortunate accident that forced you to be strong.

For instance, a child's reaction to emotional neglect can be either negative or positive. If it's negative, the neglected child will go through life looking for somebody to give him the love and care he didn't get as a youngster. He'll keep looking for the holding and cuddling because the problem of being neglected is still unresolved for him. Intellectually he doesn't recognize his problem because it's an unconscious problem he can't control. He can't help it that he still needs nurturing even 40 years after Mom pushed him away when he wanted to be hugged.

If the reaction to neglect is positive, the problem

is resolved. The kid decides, "No one else is going to take care of me so I'd better take care of myself." He got lucky when his subconscious programmed a mature attitude.

Everybody has such initial sensitizing events that force them to make emotional decisions that program thousands of attitudes in their subconscious minds.

A similar event—whether it happens hours, months, or many years later—is a stimulating event that reinforces the emotional attitude. The subconscious computer looks through its files, finds the initial sensitizing event, and says, "Yeah, that happened before. It's just as true now as it was then." Every time a stimulating event brings back the attitude, it's reinforced emphatically, like another nail in the coffin. Such attitudes will stay with you forever unless you consciously decide to change them.

Your early childhood programming began at birth when your mind was a blank tablet ready to be programmed by everything it encountered. Like a sponge, it sucked up and absorbed everything it was exposed to. The mind, defenseless during those early childhood years, believes everything it's told. A classic kid remark is: "I know it's true 'cause Mommy told me" or "Dad told me, and that makes it so." Imagine what happens to the kid when Dad loses his temper and says, "You're the stupidest kid I ever met. You're never going to amount to anything. It embarrasses me that you're my son." The kid absorbs that outburst and believes that too, just like he believes in Santa Claus.

Like everyone else, you were programmed to

believe in fantasy. When you reached a certain point in life, you realized that the Easter Bunny, Santa Claus, and the Tooth Fairy didn't exist, and you took your literal belief in them out of your computer bank.

However, many people, who didn't reject the belief in fantasy itself, continue to live their lives in a dream world. A battered wife believes maybe her husband will change. That's a fantasy. A henpecked husband believes maybe his wife will become less demanding. He's fooling himself. The belief in fantasy is still stuck in the computer bank, along with other negative childhood programming that people react to 30, 40, or 50 years later without knowing why.

Mental blocks are set up when you're a little kid, programming guilts that can bother you all your life. "Masturbating is a dirty, filthy, nasty habit. You ought to be ashamed of yourself," you probably were told. As a kid you didn't even know why you ought to be ashamed, but you were, and the guilt carries over to adulthood. Even though you probably no longer consider masturbation to be evil, if you masturbated, could you do it without guilt?

You learn early in life about the double-bind dilemma. You can't get out of a double bind, no matter what you do. When somebody says you ought to be ashamed of yourself, you feel guilty if you're not ashamed—and that's bad. If you *are* ashamed, that's bad too. If somebody tells a young mother she should quit her job and stay home with her children, she feels guilty if she keeps her job—and that's bad. If she quits the job, stays home, and feels cheated, that's bad too.

There's no way out of a double-bind dilemma, except to reprogram the emotional attutide that creates the conflict.

When you reach age five or six, you begin to develop a critical faculty, the ability to analyze whether things are true or false, the ability to learn from your own experiences, as well as the experiences of others. You develop this ability as you come to realize that people lie to you, cheat you, take advantage of you—and your critical faculty grows to defend you. You begin to analyze what is good or bad in order to look out for Number One. Nevertheless, the initial programming sticks, especially the programming to follow Mom's and Dad's rules.

A kid comes home from third grade with a test he's flunked. "Oh, you're so stupid," Mom or Dad says. "Look at how easy that is, and you couldn't even do it. You're never going to learn, are you?" The idea plugs in because it's an emotionally charged thing. Mom and Dad say we're going to have dinner, and we do. Dad says Santa will come, and he does. Mom says I'm stupid, so I am. That's a heavy-duty insecurity programmed on a computer tape that replays for years.

Years later, when the kid is grown up, his intellect tells him his parents' evaluation of his ability doesn't make sense. "I know better than that now," he tells himself. "I know better than to believe they really thought I was stupid." But he can't intellectualize the problem away. He can rid himself of his inferiority complex only if he can psych himself into reprogramming a crippling childhood attitude, just as you can learn to counter the negative programming lodged in your sub-conscious with positive programming to help you become the person you want to be.

**INSTANT RECALL:** "The past was an accident; the future is mine."

# CHAPTER 3

# Your Ongoing
# Emotional Programming

EVERY TIME YOU have a new experience, you add programming to your emotional computer bank. If you've never gone to an X-rated movie, you have no emotional reference to know how you would react. Once you've attended one, you implant programming that tells you either, "No thanks, I don't enjoy sex on the silver screen," or "Wow! That was interesting. I think I might improve my own sex life if I saw more of those."

If you've never ridden a motorcycle, you have no basis for understanding how it would feel. After your first ride, you'll know darn well if you want to repeat the experience or not. Your emotional subconscious, which received programming from that first ride, will let your conscious, intellectual mind know right away whether you consider motorcycles a terror or a thrill.

Traumas program your subconscious in the same way. By definition a trauma is an experience that damages, either physically or psychologically. But the experience is not as important as how you react to it.

If you ever have an auto accident, you will not be able to pass the scene of the accident again without thinking of it. If you fall off the ladder when you're painting the garage, you're not likely to climb it again without remembering.

Traumas keep on influencing your actions even if you can't remember them. Such was the case with Paula, who came to me for help in improving her behavior toward her husband. Paula was obsessed to do things to displease him. She would be a good wife for two weeks, but then she'd sit half the night in a bar just to make her husband angry. She'd be a good wife for another two weeks, then she'd let the dirty dishes pile up in the sink for four days because she knew he'd lose his temper.

Her spells of choosing behavior to aggravate her husband were sporadic. At other times she would be Mrs. Ideal Wife that hubby loved to come home to.

Her husband couldn't stand cursing, so she'd throw out a few dirty words now and then. Other times she'd be the model of propriety. Sometimes when she tried hard to please him, her attempt wouldn't quite make it—even when she thought she was trying her best. She painted a vase to match the living room decor, but left splotches of spray paint on the basement floor. She'd do one thing very nicely, but leave another badly screwed up.

I used hypnosis to try to find the emotion in

Paula's computer bank that caused the child in her to tamper with her adult behavior. Her mother and father had both quit high school when they had to get married. Her mother didn't want the baby because she had designs on a higher quality of life. Her father was very talented mechanically, but he was not particularly bright. He was content to go through life working with his hands.

Two more children arrived, none of them wanted by the mother. The children were always in her way. She blamed them for her own frustration, feeling they dragged her down and kept her from being happy and successful.

Once when her mother was sleeping and her father was supposed to keep the children quiet, Paula wanted to make a peanut butter sandwich. She was trying to be very quiet so as not to awaken her mother, but she made too much noise to please her father. He stomped into the kitchen, furious that Paula was making so much noise that her mother might awaken and blame him for not controlling the kids. In his anger he grabbed the peanut butter jar away from Paula and slammed it on the counter so hard it broke.

Twenty years later her subconscious remembered the episode vividly. The subconscious never forgets, although sometimes it won't yield its information to the conscious mind. The experience was traumatic to Paula. She equated the act of violence on the peanut butter jar to an act of violence on herself. She was a bad little girl. The idea programmed itself into her computer bank, and even after she was an adult, a part of her was always looking for a way to prove she was a bad little girl. The adult in her would do its good thing, but the kid in her would screw it up in the end. Just when she thought she had everything together, an unresolved emotional pattern that needed to prove she was a bad little girl popped out.

Consciously, Paula had forgotten the incident. When she recalled the incident under hypnosis, I plugged into her subconscious a different perception of what had happened. The attack on the peanut butter jar was no longer an attack on her. She matured her perception of the event so that she no longer had to be programmed to be a bad little girl, no matter what her age. I programmed her to remember only good little girl memories, even in her dreams. She had those good little girl memories within her; I just helped her to bring them out so she could be a good grown-up person.

Did Paula need a hypnotist to help her make this change? No. Had she carefully analyzed her problem, she would have recognized her behavior as the bad little child in her. To make that bad little child grow up, or to let her good child dominate the bad, she would never have to know the exact incident that programmed the bad little girl to pop out.

You, too, can change the things put into your computer by initial childhood programming and traumatic experiences. If you can pinpoint the incident that triggered the programming, you can alter your interpretation of the incident. If you can't pinpoint specific causes, you can certainly isolate the feelings you have that you don't want, and—once you recognize them as undesirable— learn to bring back good feelings that will counteract the negative programming that caused

them. You can also change programming en-
grained in your subconscious by repeating suggestions you'd like your subconscious to accept as
true.

Your subconscious will eventually accept something you habitually think over and over and over
again as you talk to yourself mentally. The
thought continues like an endless record until your
subconscious finally emotionalizes it and you
believe it.

Childhood programming of this type reminds
you that if you step on a crack you'll break your
mother's back, that it's bad luck to walk under
ladders or to have a black cat walk in front of you.
An idea repeated often enough lodges in your subconscious forever. If the idea is negative, it can
louse up your life forever, as it did with one of my
clients who was afraid to make a decision by
herself.

When she was a child, Debbie's mother always
told her, "If you don't do what I tell you, it'll be
wrong." If she didn't stack the dishes in the
drainer the way her mother told her to, she'd
break one, her mother said. Sure enough, a
favorite coffee mug slipped from its position and
shattered. If she didn't study quietly at her
bedroom desk instead of sprawled on the bed with
the hi-fi blasting, she'd flub her test. Sure enough,
Debbie got a C in literature even though she was
carrying an A until exam time.

Her mother's predictions proved to be true with
such regularity that Debbie became uptight about
deciding herself how anything should be done.
Any way except her mother's was sure to be
wrong. Even when she was a mother with teen-

agers of her own, she was incapable of making a decision without consulting her mother. What color drapes would be best in the living room? Should the sofa be placed on the long wall under the seascape or by the credenza facing the fireplace? Her subconscious continued accepting the idea that something done her own way would be wrong until she learned to psych herself into rejecting the negative idea and replacing it with a positive one. Only then was she able to cut herself off from her mother's perfectionism and do things her own way without fear of the consequences.

Repetition of positive suggestions is the principle used by Alcoholics Anonymous to help problem drinkers stay away from alcohol. *One Day at a Time*, the book read over and over by members trying to rid themselves of their addiction, says: "The program programs." More accurately, the program reprograms. Through repetition the twelve-step A program gets down to the alcoholic's subconscious and changes his emotional computer. By the time a member gets through the twelfth step, when he's then ready to help others become non-practicing alcoholics, the positive principles espoused by the program are thoroughly ingrained in his subconscious. Few members who complete all twelve steps ever return to drinking because they have developed positive emotions to a strength that can counter the negative programming that drove them to drink.

The power of positive thinking *does* work, but it's a long, drawn-out process. I can turn you on to quicker ways of programming your subconscious on purpose to change the accidental programming that controls your life.

A computer is a highly sophisticated, complicated piece of machinery that pumps out answers to problems based upon the information it's programmed with. It does the best it can on the basis of its programming. That's the way the subconscious is. On the basis of its resources—whatever it's been programmed for—it does what it thinks is best for you. On its list of emotional priorities, it computes what its language says is best. If the reaction turns out to be bad, it is the least painful of the available choices—as your subconscious sees it.

If you don't like the choices your subconscious has made, you must get new resource data in your computer bank. One method of getting new emotional references is to have new experiences for which you now have no programming. Other methods are to alter your emotional computer bank's interpretation of old experiences or to retrieve stored emotions and integrate them to present situations. Because your mind contains both the cure and the cause for any problem, you can choose your own ongoing emotional programming.

**INSTANT RECALL:** "Rotten luck won't get me stuck."

# PART TWO

# Programming to Make You What You Want to Be

# CHAPTER 4

# Choosing Emotions
# You Want

EVERY TIME I hypnotize a client, I observe firsthand how the mind works. I know two people are inside your head debating every decision you make. When one says "Go" and the other says "Stop," you've got problems you won't overcome until you get the parts of your mind working together.

The subconscious has two sections to it. The bigger section is the emotional part that feels, and the smaller is the automatic part that controls autonomic bodily functions such as breathing, heartbeat, and temperature. The automatic part never stops working. If someone says, "Roses are red," your subconscious can't help but finish the verse for you. It has sorted out everything you've consciously absorbed and programmed it into your computer, which spouts out the second line of the poem.

The two sections of the subconscious have been programmed through experiences, traumas, and repetition to make you what you really are. The subconscious is the part of your mind used to develop physical coordination and self-defense, to make esthetic judgments, to solve problems, and to appreciate art, music, and poetry. It is the creative side of your brain.

The conscious mind is the intellectual, verbal side of your mind that exercises itself constantly by thinking all the time. If you've ever tried to turn your intellectual mind off, you know it can't be done. Some thought is always floating around during every waking moment. Without fusing the conscious and subconscious minds to agree, the two parts of the mind are in conflict, and the conscious, intellectual part will almost always be the loser.

To become a competent adult instead of a bad little girl, Paula got her emotions to agree with her intellectual desire to be an efficient, lovable wife. To become a decision-maker, Debbie got her emotions to agree with her intellectual belief that she would not make mistakes as her mother had led her subconscious to believe. You, too, can learn to use both pieces of your mind cooperatively, the way they're intended to be used. Unfortunately, most people don't use their minds right. They demand things from their intellects that their intellects can't do. The intellect can figure out what needs to be done, but it can't do it unless it gets an emotional charge.

People believe if they can intellectually think, "Don't be afraid," they should be able to feel unafraid, but that's not true. Only the 10 percent of them that's intellectual wants to eliminate the fear. The 90 percent of them that's emotional will feel afraid until it flashes back to prior programming that enables them to understand that the fear is unnecessary. Only then can both parts of the mind give 100 percent cooperation in producing the desired feeling.

The subconscious is always looking for a feeling to go with a particular situation, but often it comes up with one you would not deliberately choose. It's the déjà-vu principle. Whenever anything happens to you, something similar has happened before. You've been there. Your subconscious is already seeing what being there again will be like. If the first experience was not pleasant, the feeling your subconscious chooses to go with the second will be unpleasant. The mind keeps looking for patterns to replay, and it will continue finding the old, existing ones until you help it find a new one.

For instance, if you're entertaining the boss and his wife for the first time, you intellectually want the evening to be perfect, but you might be emotionally uptight. If you are uptight, you can be certain that some similar incident in your past did not go well; otherwise you wouldn't have an uptight feeling. If you had just successfully given a dinner party which all guests enjoyed tremendously, you'd be confident you could do the same this time.

But the boss is coming, and you're uptight when you don't want to be. You want to be a relaxed, secure, happy host or hostess. What most people don't realize is they can choose to feel the way they want to feel. You don't have to get stuck with the feeling the subconscious chose for you, if you learn the simple steps of psychofusion and auto-echo.

First recognize that you don't like the uptight feeling you have. Second, be aware that you have a choice of how you feel. Third, let your intellect explore the possibilities. You have several choices. You can remain uptight, but you don't want to do that because the boss would probably notice and you wouldn't project the image you want. You could have a couple of cocktails to unwind, but you don't want to do that because you'll be serving cocktails to your guests. The last thing you want is to have one too many and run the risk of your boss's thinking you're a lush. Or you could choose to be relaxed—obviously the best of your possible choices.

Of course, intellectually telling yourself to be relaxed doesn't make you relaxed. The intellect knows what needs to be done, but it can't do it without an emotional charge. Getting that charge is the fourth step, when you say to your sub-conscious: give me the feeling of relaxation.

Follow this three-step procedure to retrieve the proper feeling from your subconscious:

First, breathe in as deeply as possible, and then exhale slowly, letting the air out in an even gradual flow.

Second, think the words, "Melt and relax," as though speaking to your body.

Because most people are too tense to make an immediate feeling change, the ability to melt and relax on cue may take practice. To master instant melting, close your eyes and roll them upward as though you can see through your forehead, and focus on a spot in the middle of your brow. As you focus on the spot, try to open your eyes. If you can open them, you're not focusing correctly, and your eyes will be looking forward instead of rolling up. Keep trying to focus on the middle of your forehead until you cannot open your eyes. The concentration needed to focus on that spot is necessary to master instant relaxation with the cue words, "Melt and relax."

After five seconds of being unable to open your eyes, take a deep breath, counting slowly downward from ten, feeling a melting relaxation, and using the same deep breath to complete the count to one. Allow your head to slowly fall toward your right shoulder.

Count downward two more times from ten, using one deep breath to deepen your level of relaxation. The more you practice this forehead-focusing relaxation technique, the closer you'll be to relaxing instantly to the cue words, "Melt and relax."

Now for the third step of psychofusion: Drift back to a time when you felt relaxed, to the memory you need to overcome your uptight feeling as a host or hostess about to entertain the boss. See the memory of your relaxed self vividly in your mind; focus on the details of the circumstances to increase your comfort. Let the same feeling you had then flow back into your mind and body.

How do you find the right memory? At first, you'll have to intellectually search your brain for a memory that contains the feeling you want. Eventually, you'll have pet memories to draw upon for particular feelings. When you want to feel relaxed, you'll automatically remember a particular sunny day on the beach when all the cares of the world seemed so far from you. When you want to feel energetic, you'll flash back immediately to a day when you awakened raring to go and accomplished your day's goals with ease.

How do you get the right feeling to flow back into your body? Most people can retrieve a feeling simply by thinking about it. Others need a tangible recall piece, such as a scrapbook, a seashell, a coin, a ring, a familiar chair—any meaningful object directly involved in the particular memory.

Touching, smelling, hearing, seeing, tasting— all the senses bring back reactions. When you smell smoke, you react with apprehension. When you hear music that was special for you and another person, you think of that person. Psychofusion uses this principle to find good feelings and reject automatic bad ones.

Once you let the proper stored feeling come to the conscious level, you can apply it to your present task. Before your boss arrives, you can become relaxed and confident because you will have your emotions and your intellect agreeing on the solution to your uptight problem. That's psychofusion.

Auto-echo will help to emotionalize the feeling you've chosen. While letting the feeling you choose flow into your body, repeat mentally the words "I am relaxed" ten times, progressively pressing each finger or thumb to keep count on your leg, your stomach, or whatever part of your body seems most comfortable. Through repetition, your subconscious will emotionalize the statement and accept it as true.

In this example the suggestion you give yourself is to be relaxed, but you can retrieve any feeling that you want from your subconscious. Psychofusion works on the same principle as looking at a scrapbook. When you look at photos taken years ago, you resurrect the memory of those years, along with the feelings that go with them. Likewise, you have an emotional scrapbook of valuable memories. Looking into that subconscious scrapbook can bring back the feel of those memories.

Psychofusion and auto-echo can be used together or separately, depending upon the circumstances. Obviously, if you become irate at a reckless driver on a busy expressway, it's impossible to close your eyes and complete the psychofusion procedure. However, you could easily employ auto-echo as you continue driving, pressing a finger or thumb each time you tell your subconscious, "I will not allow that reckless driver to control my emotions."

You can do what you intellectually want if you can get your emotions to agree on the goal. Your dreams can be realized if you can emotionalize them, as well as intellectualize them.

People think certain things will come true without emotionalizing. Students go to school assuming the teacher will make them smart. People do their jobs assuming the boss will give them a promotion. People go to church assuming God will make them good. They wait for something external to reach inside and change them.

But that's not the way to make things happen. Don't wait for something outside to reach in and change you. You've been waiting long enough for the accidents of your life to correct themselves, and nothing has happened yet. You can change those accidents only by working from the inside out. If you can get your inside, subconscious mind to agree with your outside, conscious mind—you can make whatever change you desire.

With psychofusion you can get the emotional charge you need to be able to do what you want to do. You already know what the problem is, you know what to do to solve it, but you don't feel like doing it. Until you get the feeling right, the problem won't be solved. You've got the vehicle, but you need the gas to make it run.

The gas is there in your subconscious. You've used it before, and now when you need it again, you must bring it back to the conscious level. People get the gas from their subconscious automatically in many situations. They get the emotional feeling to spur them to do what they intellectually want to do. That's why some people won't get on the dance floor until they get the feel of the music by tapping their hands and feet until they "feel" like dancing. When they go into a bar with a band, they intellectually decide to dance, but they don't do it until the music gives them the emotional charge. Many people also listen to music when they're feeling down in the dumps, knowing the music will crank them up. They don't have the feeling they want, so they get it.

That's why so many couples go to X-rated movies. Intellectually, they want to increase their sexual rapport, but they can't do it until something creates the emotional feeling they need for sexual intimacy.

Do you think as many people would answer the

altar call at the beginning as at the end of the church service? Of course not. The service itself is geared to build the emotional arousal needed to lead them to the altar.

More fights traditionally follow hockey games or football games that have been full of fights because people absorb the emotional atmosphere and become hostile themselves. They get the feeling of violence and plug it into their own situations.

The subconscious finds feelings for you all the time. Why not let it find feelings to make your life more pleasant? Why not guide it intellectually to the feeling you want? That's what you do with psychofusion.

I illustrate psychofusion hypnotically by sticking a person to a chair when he doesn't even know he's been hypnotized. This technique is known as waking hypnosis. When I tell a person he will stick to a chair, he will—not because I have the power to stick him there, but because he is ready to accept my suggestion. Experience has taught me which persons are ready to accept such a suggestion.

Being stuck is a mind-boggler for a wide-awake person who intellectually knows he should be able to stand up from the chair. The problem is that his subconscious, which has accepted my suggestion, doesn't agree that he can rise from a sitting position. Without his emotions agreeing with his intellect, he is both literally and figuratively stuck until I tell him how to get his power back. All he needs to do is close his eyes, go back in his memory to a time when he was sitting in a chair and a time when he can remember standing up from that chair. He needs to go inside that memory, watch himself stand up, and get back the feeling that he had then. Once he finds the proper feeling, he can stand up.

When a subject follows my instructions, thinks carefully, and stands up, he usually grins like crazy. He's excited because he thinks he has broken the hypnotist's power. But actually, it was the power of his subconscious that he broke. His subconscious kept him stuck to the chair until he found the proper feeling to fuse with his intellectual desire to stand up.

Until I give a subject the secret of psychofusion, he will try intellectually to change the reality of sticking to a chair. He intellectually knows he is not truly stuck, but knowing that does not help him change the reality of being stuck. His subconscious, emotional mind caused him to stick, and only his subconscious, emotional mind can unstick him.

The secret that can free you from undesirable life patterns is right there in your head, waiting for you to find it and fuse it with your intellectual desire for change. Changing yourself is like baking a cake. If you don't have the right ingredients, the finished product won't turn out right. You must find the right ingredient in the pantry to get the product you want. With that ingredient you can psych yourself to reach your goal.

**INSTANT RECALL:** "Psych, choose, feel, fuse."

# CHAPTER 5

# Making Psychofusion Work for You

YOU SKEPTICS OUT there are saying, "Psychofusion sounds good, but it'll never work." I don't blame you. Psychofusion is easy, and most people are programmed to think something easy can't have much substance to it. Like most people, you probably believe that your problems are complicated enough to require complicated solutions.

You'll never know how effective psychofusion can be until you try it. While you're initially trying it, you'll wonder, "Why should I be listening to that crazy hypnotist? What does he know about how I can change my emotions?"

I'm telling you that I do know. Now that you know the psychofusion technique, only one hang-up can prevent you from using it successfully: your own disbelief in your ability to do so. People are strange. They trust psychiatrists, psychologists, and social workers to pinpoint their problems and help them resolve them. They trust hypnotists to plug in suggestions to change them. But they don't trust themselves.

You've got to dump the insecure idea that someone else can help you, but you can't help yourself. It's *your* mind. No matter what a psychological professional does to help you, it's *you* who makes the decision either to change or remain the same. No matter what a hypnotist plugs into your subconscious, it's *you* who decides whether to let that suggestion work. All hypnosis is self-hypnosis. All help is self-help. Psychofusion *can* work for you. I see it work every day, and I've seen it work for thousands of clients.

Marvin, for instance.

Marvin came to me because he freaked out at the idea of asking a girl to dance, a common problem among young single men. Marvin said the particular girl he'd like to approach usually sat with friends all the way across the big room of the singles' bar. Intellectually he wanted to take a shot at her, but his emotions wouldn't let him. His emotions knew he'd have to walk all the way from the bar to the table where she was chatting with friends. After he got there, he would have to maneuver around the other girls—all talking incessantly and loudly to be heard above the band's blare—to isolate the one he wanted to dance with. He would have to figure out something clever to say to get her attention, and then he would have to pose the proposition of dancing. He would have to stand there waiting while the girls suddenly became silent as the desirable one contemplated her answer.

Marvin couldn't bring himself to go through the painful steps necessary to make this girl's acquaintance. He had traveled that route once before and got shot down. The girl said no, and he had to walk all the way back across the big room with everybody in the bar knowing she turned him down. Emotionally, that didn't feel good, and he wasn't crazy about having it happen again. He was intimidated by the computer programming that told him he'd get rejected.

I explained psychofusion to Marvin. ''You've got to go back in your memory to a time when you didn't get rejected. You've got to find a time in your past when someone recognized that you were nice and accepted you. You've got to find that good feeling so that every time you ask someone to dance, it's a fresh, one-time experience. You've got either to selectively reject that bad experience from your emotional computer or mature your perception of it. You can't let it continue to control your social life.''

Marvin, who was 22, was sure he had no positive-reinforcement situation to go back to. He remembered the senior prom when the bouncy cheerleader he had a crush on danced with almost every guy but him. He remembered the junior prom when he couldn't work up the nerve to ask the band's leading flutist to do the bump. But he also remembered Mary Lou, who said yes at the freshman hop and gave him the positive experience he needed to go back to. Recalling the happy feeling he had when Mary Lou saved him from embarrassment of rejection, Marvin fused that feeling with his intellectual desire to meet this particular girl at the singles' bar.

The guy without a Mary Lou needs to go back further, even if it's way back to fifth grade when he was chosen first for a spelling match. It's the rare person who can't find some positive emotional experience in his past.

First, determine the emotion you need to achieve what you intellectually want. Relax and go back in your memory to a time when you had that feeling. Remember the positive experience that caused you to feel the way you need to feel now. Let the thought of that memory flood into your head. Visualize it. Feel it. Step inside and relive the feeling.

Reject other conflicting feelings. The last 15 times when girls turned Marvin down and he had to walk across that big room thinking everyone knew he was rejected—those last 15 times don't count. If he cannot selectively reject the feeling of failure from his emotional computer, Marvin can at least mature his reaction to being turned down.

Because every experience he's ever had will always be stored in his subconscious, he may be unable to keep the memory from popping up, but he can change his perception of the memory. He can realize that being turned down for a dance doesn't make him a social outcast. He should feel grateful in a way. By telling him no the first time, those girls saved him a lot of time and money and kept him from making any emotional investment in them. He didn't get anything positive from the experience, but he doesn't have to take away anything negative either. Besides, he can remember Mary Lou. She recognized his good qualities, so there's no doubt he has some.

With that kind of reasoning, Marvin can repro-

gram his subconscious. He may not eliminate the
memory, but he can mature his perception of it.

Bryan, however, needed new programming
because he had absolutely no positive male-female
experience in his past. As much as he tried, he
could find nothing positive to remember about his
relationship with girls.

"Do you accept the fact that we have to have a
positive base experience to work from?" I asked,
after explaining the psychofusion technique.

He did.

"Do you think there are other people in the
world who feel like you? Or do you think you're
the only one who's ever been afraid of being embarrassed by being turned down by a girl?"

He knew he wasn't.

"How about those girls, then? Do you think
any girls in the world feel just like you? Do you
think any girls sit around at dances wishing some
guy would ask them to dance, but never getting
the opportunity to say yes to anyone?"

He admitted such girls existed and that he could
identify with their feelings.

"I want you to ask those girls to dance. If
they're ugly, what does that matter? If they're
losers, who cares? I want you to ask them to dance
because you're going to give those people a feeling
of acceptance and pride. You know how important that is to a person because you don't have it
right now yourself. You're feeling like you're not
such a red hot guy just because some girls who
didn't know how to judge character or value
turned you down. But you're a clean-cut guy, an
honest guy—aren't you? You look pretty good,
don't you? You're going to ask those ugly girls to

dance to give them some pleasure.

"If you do, you'll give those girls, who lead such dull lives, a feeling of acceptance and pride. Do you think you can give that feeling to someone else? Did you ever do that? Did you ever feed your dog and have him lick your hand to love you? Did you ever give someone a present at Christmas and make them happy as hell? You did? Good! You know what it feels like then. It feels good to make someone else happy.

"Tonight you're going to give happiness to somebody else. Maybe it doesn't sound good when I tell you you're going to dance with homely girls, but it's going to feel good. And it's going to feel good to them. Can you do that? You admit we have to have a positive base experience to work from, and we've got to start somewhere. Besides, you'll be amazed how many not-so-hot girls are really nice people."

Bryan danced with them. He began to get the feeling that people appreciated him. He began to realize he really was acceptable after all. He accumulated positive experiences for his emotional computer bank. He accepted that if anybody rejected him, it wasn't because something was wrong with him. Too many others had accepted him for him to let that worry him. He didn't have the feeling he needed, so he got it by seeking new experiences.

That's the secret of change. If you don't have the needed feeling to fuse with your intellectual desire to change, go get it. That means trying out new things, and that's scary to a lot of people. It's tough, but anything tough is a character-builder.

A woman who came to me to reprogram her attitude toward her brother also needed to change her perception of past events. Zelda wanted me to hypnotize her and tell her she'd be able to get along with her brother, whom she actually detested. That's what most hypnotists do; they plug in symptom removal suggestions, but they don't do anything about the problem itself. They don't mesh or mature or complement or improve the old attitudes and old feelings. Even if symptom removal suggestions are plugged into the subconscious, the old attitudes and old feelings are still there, the same as they were before. You can't just ignore them, cover them up, or repress them—that doesn't work, as I explained to Zelda.

"You want me to zap you and tell you your brother's a wonderful person, and you'll be able to talk to him from now on with no problem at all," I told her. "Does that sound like it's going to solve the problem?"

She admitted it did not, that she'd still remember the time her brother hit her with a board, and the time he told her parents she was running around with the gas station attendant, and the time he squealed on her for smoking in the john.

"What about that?" I asked. "You'll still remember those times, so when I tell you he's cool, and you're going to communicate and be comfortable with him—that doesn't fit too well, does it? You've got a whole bunch of stored-up experiences screaming at you that he's a rat, and it won't work to ignore them. Your head won't buy it if you just tell your subconscious he's lovable and you can get along with him now. Wrong. Your head may buy it for a little while, but there are too many past experiences shouting, 'No, no—this doesn't fit. It conflicts with everything I've experienced with my brother.' Pretty soon those old memories will burst through and bury the new suggestion, and you'll be right back where you started—hating your brother.''

Zelda thought I was probably right.

"We've got to start with your realizing it's okay to feel the way you feel about your brother," I said. "You don't have to feel guilty about it because he was a big jerk to hit you with a board and to squeal on you to your parents every time he caught you breaking their rules. I can understand that you hate him. But how can we improve your feeling for him now—20 years later? We're going to start on the basis that he was a little kid like you when he did little kid mean things to you. And that's okay too. You can understand that now, as an adult. Twenty years later you can understand how little kids do things to get attention. You can understand that you were the prettiest, nicest girl in the neighborhood, and your parents adored you, and he was jealous of that. Can you understand why he would feel that way? But let's come forward in time. Let's outgrow your emotional attitude of hating him on the basis that you and he are not kids anymore. Don't punish his adult for what his kid did.''

Zelda understood that she needed either to change her perception of the past, or to selectively reject her feelings toward experiences that caused her to hate her brother.

"Now, go back to a time when your brother did something you really liked, something you appreciated," I said. "Search through your memory until you find a time when you felt good about your brother.''

Zelda remembered when he saved three weeks of his paper route money to buy her a pair of roller skates for her birthday. She remembered the good feeling she had when she opened the present, the love she felt for him because he sacrificed chocolate sodas and his favorite comic books to buy her the skates she wanted.

''Go with that feeling. Get inside it and relive it. See it vividly in your mind. From now on that feeling is going to be the way you feel about your brother. Any time you start having bad thoughts about him, you're going to flash that happy memory in your mind and let its feeling flood your body. You're going to be able to accept your brother because he's a human being—even though he's immature in certain areas, just as you are. But even when he does something you don't like, you can have this gut level feeling that he has a good side too. Practice treating him as an adult, instead of treating him like you treated the kid. Practice. Appreciate it when he does something good. When he does something bad, accept it as the child part coming out of him, and that's okay. He needs to mature in certain areas, and maybe you do too. But you've matured your attitude toward your brother. You've changed your perception of experiences that kept you hating him as an adult because of things he did as a kid.''

If you have very strong attitudes, you can't ignore or repress them, but you can always reconsider them by looking at the experiences that caused the attitudes through 26-year-old eyes instead of 12-year-old eyes. Then follow the psychofusion steps. Find a time in your past when you had a different attitude, and plug it into your present situation. The psychofusion technique works for accomplishing changes you want.

**INSTANT RECALL:** "I see yesterday better through today's eyes."

# CHAPTER 6

# Testing Your
# Emotional Flexibility

THERE'S NO QUESTION that psychofusion works.
The only question is how easily it will work for
you, as an individual. You would face the same
question if you came to me wanting to use hypnosis to reprogram a specific personal habit.
There's no question that hypnosis works for such
reprogramming. The only question is how recep-
tive you might be to hypnosis because your receptivity would determine how quickly the reprogramming would work.

Some people are natural subjects, but others
must learn to respond to hypnosis. The same is
true of psychofusion. To determine your respon-
siveness to psychofusion, answer yes or no to the
following questions:

1. Do you believe faith healing is possible?

2. Do you consider yourself a religious person?

3. Do you feel hypnosis could help you solve a problem?

4. Do you find magic shows or ESP fascinating?

5. Do you get angry easily or feel emotions quickly?

6. Do you often speak too quickly or off the top of your head, and regret it?

7. Are you able to enjoy sitting still for periods of 20 to 30 minutes?

8. Do you usually trust what people tell you?

9. Do you go to sleep easily at night?

10. Do you enjoy reading or going to movies?

11. Do you consider yourself imaginative or creative?

12. Do you consider yourself a calm person?

13. Do you have blonde or dark hair with blue, gray, or green eyes?

14. Do you ever walk or talk in your sleep?

15. Do you think learning to relax would be important to your health?

16. Do you wish you could avoid taking any medicine?

17. Do you daydream often of better ways to do things?

18. Do you prefer fictional stories to nonfictional articles?

19. Do you remember ever being afraid of the dark or heights?

20. Do you remember your dreams?

Your test score should be a good indication of how easy psychofusion will be for you, but keep in mind that no test is 100 percent valid.

Generally speaking, if you have from 14 to 20 yes answers, you are an excellent subject for psychofusion, capable of reprogramming your emotional subconscious mind the way you want it to be instead of the way it turned out by accident. If you have from 9 to 13 yes answers, you're a potentially good subject, but you need to relax and develop an effortless concentration. Don't try—just let it happen, considering psychofusion as a personal pleasure leading to positive change.

If you have from 4 to 8 yes answers, you will be able to use psychofusion, but only after you practice emotional receptivity. Start by training yourself to concentrate on an emotion you want to feel. Happiness, hate, love, or fear—think it over and over until you feel it inside and see a memory picture of it in your mind.

As another exercise, remember a location you loved to visit. See it in your mind, with every possible detail. If it's a beach, visualize the waves breaking against the sand, the grooves formed as the sand sweeps out toward the ocean, curving around broken seashells or even a discarded pop bottle. Remember the blueness of the sky, the way puffy white clouds floated effortlessly over the crystal water, the flick of a white sail as it disappeared over the horizon.

In your continuous effort to improve your ability to concentrate, learn to play games with the alphabet. When you're meeting so many people that you would ordinarily never remember their names, place them mentally on the alphabet. Soon after placing them in their correct slots, start mentally saying the alphabet from A to Z. After saying each letter to yourself, blank your mind and relax until the person's name comes to your mind. You can use alphabet concentration for many tasks— from memorizing your grocery list to memorizing the topics and subtopics of a speech you must present before your superiors.

To become good at practicing psychofusion, you must also learn to exercise your imagination. As you listen to music, invent a story with a plot to fit the particular rhythm and melody. When you look at a painting, imagine a scene from a movie taking place on the canvas at that moment. When you look at a photograph, conjure up the reasons the photographer felt that particular scene worth capturing. Enjoy your imagination. Get in touch with your feelings without critical judgment.

If you have less than 4 yes answers on this test, you will have a very difficult time mastering psychofusion. You probably are suspicious, un-trusting, and analytical. To learn to use psychofusion to change yourself, you must learn the emotional flexibility you will need to change. Rigid personalities must bend to grow.

In general, the more trusting, creative, and imaginative a person is, the more capable he will be of using psychofusion. A fidgety worrier who is compulsive about doing things just right may be too inhibited to relax and let psychofusion happen.

Psychofusion is a step beyond hypnosis. It's hypnosis improved. I previously used only hypnosis to help people reprogram their emotional, subconscious minds that kept them hooked to hassles, but after 12 years of practicing hyp-notherapy and after working clinically with more than 30,000 people, I've discovered psychofusion is a better way to help people make the life changes they desire.

In the first place, psychofusion is a technique you can use by yourself. To use hypnosis, you need to see a hypnotherapist. Most hypnotherapists would zap you and plug in suggestions your subconscious needs to make the changes you desire. That technique doesn't work very well for long-term change because there's no emotional maturity development or advancement and no integration of the suggestion into your life. The suggestion must be fused with the total problem if it is to be effective.

If you want to give up smoking, most hypnotists would tell you cigarettes taste like burning garbage and rubber bands, and that you'll never want to smoke again. Bang. They ignore the fact that never wanting to smoke again has nothing to do with the taste of cigarettes. It has to do with the feel of the cigarette, the socializing with other people smoking and drinking coffee or alcohol, or defending yourself when somebody's arguing with you, and hundreds of other reasons—none having to do with how a cigarette tastes.

The hypnotist's suggestion might make your cigarettes taste lousy but it wouldn't keep you from wanting to smoke. Before that happens you have to improve your emotional attitude toward cigarettes and make your emotions agree with your intellectual desire to stop smoking. Unless you can fuse your emotional needs with your logical, rational idea, giving up cigarettes won't feel good. Being a non-smoker won't fit your life right. You can cram a round peg into a square hole if the round peg is small enough and you don't mind hammering it in, but it's never going to fit right. It hasn't been meshed with the square hole. It hasn't been fused with the total problem.

When a hypnotist plugs in a suggestion without fusing it with the total problem, it's like banging a nail into a shutter to hold it to a house. That's fine for a little while, but before long the shutter is going to fall off. Banging in one nail is not the proper way to tackle the problem.

Okay. I've convinced you. You want to try psychofusion to change your life. Now you must master the technique, and that takes practice on a day-to-day basis. Because almost everyone faces stress several times a day, I've found the best way for persons to master psychofusion is to practice it whenever they need to overcome stress.

Whenever anxiety gives you an uptight feeling, learn to replace it with a feeling of relaxation by following this psychofusion exercise:

First, breath in as deeply as possible and then exhale slowly and gradually.

Second, think the words, "melt and relax," as though speaking to your body.

Third, focus your mind on a memory image that makes you feel comfortable.

Before trying this technique, take the time to go back into your memory and visualize something that invariably relaxes you and makes you content. Do you love listening to the ocean? To music? Walking alone in the woods? Studying stars at night? Watching a sunset? Being with the family at Christmas or Chanukah?

Select a memory that floods only happy thoughts into your head. See it in your mind. Feel it. Step inside and relive the feelings.

If you are going to learn to relax on cue, that memory will become a part of your daily routine. You must know the memory intimately enough for it to pop into your head spontaneously with the thought cue, "melt and relax." It must be vivid enough to give you a gut-level, pleasant warm feeling.

Anytime you feel tension overtaking you, inhale deeply, exhale slowly, think "melt and relax," and visualize your pleasurable memory. Repeat three times. If you practice this technique regularly, you'll find it disrupts the development of stressful situations and prevents them from overwhelming your peace of mind.

Even if the test in this chapter indicates you will have difficulty using psychofusion, practice this particular exercise. It's possible to learn new skills for which you have little aptitude if only you have the dedication and perseverance to keep trying.

When practiced for 20 consecutive days, this technique  can become an established habitual reaction to the onset of anxiety. You will be able to psych yourself to serenity any time you choose.

If you're an executive, you'll be able to relax even when your job is on the line if your decision blows a company contract. If you're a senior taking a final exam in your most difficult subject, you'll be able to relax even though your graduation hinges upon your passing.

If you're a parent, you won't feel harried even when the three-year-old throws his spaghetti on the floor, the baby wails for his noontime bottle, and the first grader unexpectedly brings three classmates home for lunch.

Master psychofusion for everyday serenity, and you can master it to make whatever changes you desire in your life. Psychofusion pulls your mental parts together, making them teammates instead of opponents. Psychofusion can make you a winner.

**INSTANT RECALL:** "Melt, relax, and turn on my best."

# CHAPTER 7

# Rejecting Negative Programming

BECAUSE YOU HAVE every possible human emotion within you, you need not be confined to negative programming that keeps you unhappy. Emotions are like talents. You have them, but they don't grow unless you practice them. You might know how to play piano, but you need to play every day to improve your skill. You might know how to type, but try staying away from a typewriter for two years and see how accurately your fingers move then. Emotions are the same way. You've got them all, but some positive ones are so weak that negative ones overpower them. You need to practice the positive ones regularly to keep the negative ones from popping out of your emotional computer bank.

Negative programming made Ray a stutterer for most of his life. When he came to my office, he stuttered so badly he couldn't even tell the receptionist the time of his appointment. Once in my office, he attempted to describe the different kinds of help he had tried to overcome his stuttering, but he couldn't make himself clear with his painfully staggered speech. I leaned him back in a reclining chair and started a hypnotic induction. In just about 10 seconds, he was out like a light. He was a great subject—dynamite.

I age-regressed him to find out when he started stuttering and discovered it began when he was six years old. When his grandmother wouldn't let him go to town with her, he threw a temper tantrum, and she slapped him. Ray became so upset he couldn't talk, and he began to stutter after that. With his stuttering, he was trying to get people to stay with him to hear his point of view. He knew if he took longer to talk, they'd not leave him the way his grandmother did.

We reprogrammed his attitude as a six-year-old kid by having him view the episode through his 23-year-old eyes.

"Your grandmother really loved you and cared about you, don't you think?" I asked him. "She lost her temper because she was an old lady, and she felt you shouldn't be allowed to throw a temper tantrum without some punishment. She didn't want to take you to town because she was trying to do the best thing for you at the time. She was protecting you from things you didn't need to be involved in when you were six years old. You must see now, at age 23, that you don't have to stutter any longer to get people's attention. People can like you for yourself and want to stay with you for your good qualities not just because you take so long to talk."

After growing up his programmed six-year-old perception of the incident, we took Ray back to a time when he didn't stutter so he could get inside that feeling and apply it to the present. After I brought him back through the years until the present and woke him up, he said, "Boy, that's amazing. I haven't thought about that for years."

The sentence came out without a single stammer. He couldn't believe it. After he paid his bill to the receptionist, she came into my office and said, "What happened in here with that guy?" He couldn't even talk when he walked into this office."

I told Ray if he ever stuttered again to come back to see me. That was three years ago, and I haven't heard from him since.

Could Ray have cured his stuttering with psychofusion? Absolutely. Many former stutterers who never went to hypnotists speak plainly now. If you asked them how they cured their stuttering problem, they'd probably tell you they simply outgrew it, and that's true. They came to a point in their lives that they were able to look upon the stuttering as a childish reaction that was no longer appropriate for them as adults. Knowing the exact episode that initially prompted the stuttering isn't important, but recognizing such a bad habit as a child-like pattern is.

People who solve their stuttering problems on their own use the psychofusion principle by accident, just as you use it accidentally every day. When the sun shines, you're automatically in a better mood than when the weather is rainy and dreary. With psychofusion, you can put sunshine in your life whenever you choose it.

Psychofusion would have worked with Amanda, a client whose negative programming resulted in a cough which three doctors had been unable to diagnose. None could find a reason for the cough, which was not helped by medication.

When she was referred to me, I age-regressed her, taking her back in her memory to a time when the cough started. She remembered that it began when a bite of roast beef got stuck in her throat as she tried to swallow it. Although terrified that she was choking, she managed to cough the roast beef from her throat.

Even though the incident happened six weeks previously, her subconscious was still afraid she might choke. Because she got rid of the choking problem by coughing six weeks ago, her subconscious continued the coughing to reinforce her safety. She needed her perception of the choking incident qualified so that she understood it was a one-time, isolated event. After doing that, I took her back to a feeling when she could breathe, talk, and swallow comfortably so that she could plug that feeling into the present. The coughing that had perplexed three doctors stopped immediately.

Amanda contended she would have coughed for life if not for me, and she may have—but not because she didn't have the ability to eliminate her cough with psychofusion. Even if she never traced the origin of the cough to the roast beef incident, she could recognize the problem as an erroneous interpretation of the subconscious. After all, three doctors had told her the cough was psychosomatic. What the mind has caused, the mind can cure.

Most negative programming cannot be traced

back to a single incident, as in Ray's and Amanda's cases. For instance, programming that causes students to hate studying is usually the result of cumulative classroom occurrences. Few students can look back upon one particular incident and say, "Oh, yeah, it was that third grade teacher that did me in. I haven't paid attention in class since."

Derrick, a good-looking 16-year-old athlete, had a study problem. With his great body development, he excelled at playing football and basketball, but he had trouble making his grades to stay eligible for high school competitive sports. His problem was not brains, but the fact that he could not muster up any enthusiasm for scholastic pursuits.

Intellectually wanting to improve his grades so he could be admitted to college and continue his sports career was not enough to change his attitude. His emotional dislike of classroom confinement, and requirements to study things he did not enjoy was stronger than his intellectual desire to improve his grade point average. When the intellect and the emotions are in conflict, the emotions almost always win.

To solve his dilemma, Derrick used psychofusion to make his emotions agree with his intellect. When he felt his mind wandering from a boring subject in the classroom, he'd flash back in his memory to a particular incident when he felt great pride in his good looks and athletic ability. He retrieved that proud, happy feeling from his subconscious and repeated "I'm proud to be learning" to reprogram his subconscious anti-study attitude with auto-echo. The method worked! He was able to retrieve that proud, happy feeling from his subconscious and apply it to his desire to make better grades. Whenever tempted to gaze out the classroom window rather than work geometry problems, he flashed back to that particular memory and transferred that feeling of pride into educational growth. His grades improved.

Another one of my clients absorbed negative input when he, at age 14, beat his older brother in a golf tournament. His mother shamed him for it. "You made your own brother look bad," she told him. "You shouldn't have done that. He's older than you. He should be the winner."

At age 28 when Mac was golfing professionally, he couldn't understand why he nearly always fell apart in tournaments. On certain days he could hit a ball brilliantly and make putts that would make the gallery gasp. But before the round was over, he would slice, overshoot the green, and become so embarrassed he could barely finish eighteen holes.

When he first joined the pro golf circuit, his mother repeatedly asked him, "When are you going to get a job?" Both ideas programmed themselves into his emotions: It's bad to beat someone who's older than you are, and it's bad to be on the links playing games instead of holding down a job that's really work.

Intellectually he recognized the fallacy of his feelings, but emotionally he couldn't control them. While trying to shoot his best game of golf, his 90 percent inner voice kept telling him that earning a living on a golf course was foolish, compared to holding down a real live, respectable job. No one wants to be good at something foolish.

Especially when competing against an older opponent, that inner voice outmatched his intellectual desire to win.

Through hypnotic suggestions I helped him improve his perception of golf and winning so he was able to golf well consistently. I didn't give him anything he didn't already have. His ability to golf was there—I just helped him bring it out.

Fortunately sportsmen need not pinpoint specific past self-defeating perceptions that prevent them from excelling at their sports. Psychofusion works beautifully for any sportsman. Olympic athletes call it mind practicing. They simply see themselves performing at their best and allow their subconscious minds to guide them to imitate what they see. Just as with psychofusion, they flash back to a positive memory and apply the feeling of that memory to their present situation to bring out their ingrained abilities.

You too can learn to bring out your ingrained abilities. You don't have to be stuck with negative programming you didn't choose and don't want. You can replace it with programming you choose, to eliminate accidental emotions from your life.

Turn on your best emotions, and practice them over and over. Turn off your worst emotions, and let your best overpower them. If you practice and practice, you'll eventually find that the first emotion your subconscious pops out will be a positive one. Then you'll know that you've successfully reprogrammed your emotional computer bank.

**INSTANT RECALL:** "Use it, or lose it."

# CHAPTER 8

# Programming with New Experiences

YOU WANT TO CHANGE. Somehow your life doesn't feel right, and you'd like to make it better. If you aren't certain what specific change you'd like to make, welcome to Normal City. The residents here are all dissatisfied with themselves, but they aren't certain what would make their lives better.

If you feel the same, don't worry about it. Right now you may not have the capacity to determine what change would be right for you. You may not have had the experiences that will give you the correct answer. That's why you don't have an emotional charge that makes you want to accomplish a particular change.

You need new programming to give you a more varied base of references for both your emotional and intellectual decisions. Until you get it, don't undertake any rash changes that might still leave you dissatisfied. Just continue doing whatever you're doing now, and do it the best you can. Always be aware that you're looking for something else. Go get new experiences, and sit back and analyze them, feel them, play with them. Listen to people, watch people, try new hobbies. When something feels right to you, try it.

Are you afraid to change the rules that have always governed your life? If so, start with something safe. Change your hair. It will change the way you look, and that may change the way people treat you. On the other hand, maybe no one will even notice the difference, and that's going to cause a different emotional response inside you, isn't it?

Whether you realize it or not, you have just confronted and dealt with fear. Wasn't bad, was it? From that first experience of changing your rules, you'll find it easier to change the next. Try wearing something you normally would never wear.

Some changes are harder to make than others. You can climb a half-mile hill pretty easily, but wait until you try climbing a two-mile hill. It's tough, but that's life. You just keep working on it until you get to the top of the hill. If the path is too difficult to forge, you find another route.

You'll never know what route will get you where you want to go until you test out new experiences. Any time you go to a higher level of existence and undertake a new experience—if you get a better job, move into a new neighborhood, start dating a girl or guy who used to intimidate you—you've got to change the old rules that controlled your life. The old rules no longer fit, and you must find out what the new rules are and learn to live with them.

Ralph's problem was that he lived by the old rules. When he came to me, he had already been in and out of Eloise Hospital with four suicide attempts. Psychiatrists there had tried to pinpoint why he wanted to die, and chances are it was because his brother—his hero—had killed himself in the 1950s. However, why he wanted to kill himself doesn't really matter. Many times people know why they persist in self-defeating behavior, but they keep on doing it anyway. The old Freudian approach might help you figure out the reason for something, but it doesn't do a thing to help you change your emotional priorities. A suicidal person doesn't say, "Oh, yeah, now that I know why I'd rather be dead, I won't jump off any more bridges." A suicidal person needs his priorities rearranged to feel the way he wants them to feel—emotionally, not intellectually.

Ralph had greasy hair slicked back in a style reminiscent of *Bye Bye Birdie*. He wore baggy pegged pants with a double-breasted jacket straight out of an old Jimmy Cagney movie. You had only to look at him to know he was regressively living back in the 1950s when his brother was alive. He had no job, no friends, and what little money he had could barely pay for his room and board at the YMCA.

Ralph blamed his parents for his brother's suicide, because they rejected him for his lifestyle as a musician who played saxophone in a bar band and ran around with "loose" women. Ralph's conjecture was that his brother decided to check out because his parents would no longer accept him.

Now he was convinced his parents were also trying to kill him. Although he didn't mind killing himself—he kept trying it over and over—he didn't want to be murdered by his parents, who he suspected were trying to poison him. After eating food at their house, he would get violently ill, and all the psychotherapists he'd consulted could not convince him the problem was psychosomatic.

"I'll tell you what we'll do," I told him. "You bring me the food. If I die, then you'll know it's true—your parents really are trying to do you in. If I don't get sick or die, then you'll know you're wrong, and all those psychotherapists who've told you the problem is in your head are right."

First he brought a half eaten over-ripe banana that had given him nausea, and I swallowed it in his presence. Then it was stale cookies which he thought were spiked with arsenic, and I ate them all. As time passed, he brought a variety of fruits, which he was convinced were sprayed with poison. One time I even took a swig of hand lotion which had made him sick after he put it on his hands and accidentally got some in his mouth.

After I'd eaten all these things and was still alive and kicking, he finally decided that maybe he was wrong—his parents weren't trying to kill him. Only then did we tackle the problem of his appearance.

Because my philosophy is that hurting a person can often help, I spared no words with Ralph when I told him the truth about his appearance. "You look weird, and if you're going to change,

we've got to change that," I told him. "You've
got to get a hairstyle that's not Vaseline City.
You've got to get stylish clothes and metal-
rimmed glasses instead of those horn-rims that
hide your eyebrows."

We went shopping together. Overnight his
appearance changed, but it took him three years
to become accustomed to looking good. He
couldn't believe it. His total transformation took
seven years, but he made it by seeking new experiences.

He hadn't had a date in 10 years, so he took
dancing lessons and started meeting women. He
didn't know how to talk to them, but he tried—
and learned from his mistakes. On the job scene
he began by only mowing lawns, but he progressed
to a full-time factory job. He started going to
ballgames and movies and spending hours in the
library just browsing.

I was recently best man at his wedding, when he
married an introverted but nice woman very much
like himself. Seven years before he was a total reject who felt he didn't deserve any more out of
life. Today he has a job, a wife he loves, a house
he's buying, and a baby on the way.

Ralph succeeded in changing his life by rejecting
his old rules. People who find it difficult or impossible to change their lives insist on sticking to
their old rules. They take their lunch in a brown
paper bag when everyone else on the new job eats
at the company cafeteria. They take a date to a
diner rather than try a first class restaurant where
they might feel out of place. They stick to the old
rules instead of finding out what the new rules are
and following them. They stick to the sub-

conscious programming they got by accident instead of trying new experiences to reprogram their emotional computers the way they choose.

Change your rules by seeking new experiences. Try one new experience each day, just to see how it feels. With every new experience, you grow. You *choose* something in your life instead of waiting for accidents to choose things for you.

With every new experience, you come closer to finding the change you need to make your life feel right. As you charge yourself with new experiences, you'll find yourself getting a bigger charge out of life. Why stay down in the pits when you can climb to the peak?

**INSTANT RECALL:** "I can get what I need to succeed."

# CHAPTER 9

# Rewriting the Rules of Reality

MOST PEOPLE THINK they can't change the rules of reality. No matter how much they psych themselves, they think their particular problem can't be changed. The problem is there, it's always been there, and it's always going to be there because it's reality, and reality can't be changed.

Wrong.

Reality *can* be changed. The average Peoples Temple member who followed Jim Jones to a new life in Guyana was a poor person struggling to eke out an existence, to pay meager rent, and to have food on the table. Is it reality that such a person would give one-fourth of his limited income to Jim Jones? Many did.

Others who moved into the Temple turned over all their salaries to Jones, content to live on the $2 weekly allowances he gave them. One such woman gave Jones's church her $1,000 monthly salary for nine years in return for a room and meals in his commune. Is that reality?

Is it reality that his followers did not rebel when Jones took them to the steamy climate of Guyana where they struggled for survival among poisonous snakes, rats, and jungle mosquitoes?

The Peoples Temple members were ripe for change. Jones interjected the emotional charge they needed to change their lives, and the emotional charge changed reality.

As some 900 of them drank Kool-Aid spiked with cyanide, the reality was this: Committing mass suicide accomplished nothing constructive. It caused grief to relatives and most caring Americans who found it difficult to fathom such a blind, unintelligent act. In reality, the action was dumb. If the group indeed had some need to create a new society, killing off the society's population was not the way to do it. The suicide forced a gruesome task on those obliged to clear the stacks of bodies from the site, and it forced a financial burden on our government which paid for airlifting the remains back to the United States.

The reality is that most of those suicide victims knew intellectually they were doing an unintelligent, meaningless, ridiculous thing. But an emotional charge—a higher than life need of spiritual fulfillment—changed that reality.

Although evidence indicates Jones administered drugs to his followers to keep them passive enough to follow his commands, he most likely also used the emotional persuasion of the old "world-is-crap" approach. "The world is crap, and there's only one thing you can do to save it. Leave it. If you leave it, that will prove you recognize all these earthly things as low level, and if you recognize that, you're qualified to go to a higher place. If you're willing to leave this world, then you must be ready for the next one, where there's eternal life."

Eternal life beats the hell out of three score and ten. What would you prefer—to live forever, or to live just seventy years? I'll take forever, thank you. That's the gut-level emotion of persons who set fire to their bodies to demonstrate against society's evils or fast themselves to death for a cause. They do totally irrational, unbelievable things because they're betting on eternal life. It's the ultimate of the "pay-now, play-later" concept. Pay now, and later you get your goodies, the promise of heaven. Die now, live later. Bet a few years against forever. It's a good bet if you believe it. For people who take this bet, eternity versus three score and ten is not much of a contest.

We may never know the true story of Guyana, but we can be certain Jim Jones knew the power of an emotional charge. The same kind of emotional charge caused the Charles Manson followers to shoot, stab, and bludgeon seven people to death in Los Angeles. What about Richard Speck? Do you suppose he *intellectually* wanted to murder all those nurses in Chicago? Would he take some kind of pride in saying, "Look, Ma, aren't you pleased with me? I'm a mass murderer!"

When San Francisco Mayor George Moscone wouldn't give Supervisor Dan White his job back, do you suppose White told himself, "Well, I'll just pull a gun from my pocket and shoot the guy.

If I assassinate that man, my problems will be solved. I'll get my job back, and life can go on the way it always was before"? And what logic was there in his slaying Harvey Milk? "You're homosexual, Harvey, and I don't like homosexuals, so if I shoot you, that's one less person in the world that I don't like, so I can go on being happy, happy, happy"—is that the way White thought? Of course not. Intellectualizing his problem didn't turn him into a killer. An emotional charge pulled the trigger.

Reality can only be changed emotionally, not intellectually. It cannot be changed intellectually because an intellectual reality is only a perception which you feel emotionally.

For instance, I might say to you, "You're ugly. You've got bad teeth and a terrible smile. Your nose is crooked, and your hair looks like it hasn't been shampooed in nine weeks. I don't even like to look at you, you're so repulsive."

You would be insulted. You might say, "I don't care what you think of me," but saying it doesn't change anything if you still *feel* that you care. Intellectually saying you don't care doesn't make you not care. Only an emotion can change reality.

Madison Avenue certainly understands the power of the subconscious mind. That's why advertising sells the sizzle, not the steak. Automobiles are advertised with sexy girls driving them, stroking them, or seductively stretching their bodies across their sleek, shiny surfaces. Even the dullest person realizes the sexy girl has nothing to do with how much mileage the car gets, the amount of luggage the trunk holds, or the engine efficiency for city driving. Does any woman actually feel if she drives that particular combination of chrome and steel, she'll become like the girl in the commercial? Does any man actually think he can attract such a girl if he puts himself in that particular driver's seat? Not intellectually, they don't. Emotionally, it's a different ballgame.

Lane Bryant has thin models. The store sells fat women's clothes, but they have thin models. Now—what kind of sense does that make? It makes a lot of sense if you're fat because you don't want to be fat. You want to look like that person who's modeling the Lane Bryant clothes. When fat women see Farrah Fawcett doing an exercise club ad, it feels good to them emotionally to think they could be like her. The subconscious blocks out the intellectual fact that the odds of it happening are 500,000 to one.

When a beautiful blonde Norwegian wearing a lowcut blouse tells you to "take it all off," most viewers are unconcerned about the shave cream she's selling. It doesn't take a genius to know what subconscious element that ad writer is steering toward, but most people say, "I don't fall for that. I don't believe that." What they don't realize is that the ad writer doesn't want them to believe it: he wants them to *feel* it. He wants that ad to make you *feel* like you need something even if you intellectually know you do not. Medicine cabinets brimming with unused cough syrups, pain killers, and beauty aids are testimony that the technique works.

The technique works because it employs the old American proverb: "If you want to con someone, you must first get him to trust you, or at least feel superior to you." The advertising writers deliberately make TV commercials foolish and ridiculous. They want your intellectual, conscious mind to think they are ineffective because they know your intellect won't make you change from one headache remedy to another. Only your emotional, subconscious mind will accomplish that.

Writers want their selling message to insult your intelligence so that your conscious mind thinks it cannot be swayed. They're aiming at the 90 percent of you that controls your buying decisions whether you realize it or not. Some commercials that TV viewers consider the most inane have sold their products the best. You think the reality is that TV commercials have no effect on you, but a direct appeal to your subconscious can change that reality.

That's why movie goers bought a record number of soft drinks while watching *Lawrence of Arabia*, and swimmers avoided ocean beaches after seeing *Jaws*. They bought the subconscious message. Their intellects told them they had no reason to be thirsty and no reason to fear beaches, but their emotions had no such reasoning power.

The subconscious never goes to sleep, even when the conscious mind thinks it is not listening and even when a person is physically sleeping. Patients under anesthetics have misinterpreted conversations in the operating room with deadly results. A patient might die while having a simple appendectomy just because the surgeon said, "He's all done"—meaning the doctor is ready for his assistant to close the incision. If the subconscious interpreted the sentence to mean he was dying, the patient might oblige. Operating room staffs are cautioned to be careful with the innuendos of their language because the subconscious's interpretation of what's happening can turn a simple operation into a life-or-death drama. It can change reality.

Reality is not reality if you interject an emotional charge to change it. The key to making the change you want in your life is finding the emotional charge that's right for you. Then when you are ripe for change, you can not only reject the rules of your old reality, you can break in the new reality you want.

**INSTANT RECALL:** "The only thing real is what I feel."

# CHAPTER 10

# Testing Your Realities

WHAT IS REALLY REAL?

The Federal Food and Drug Administration says laetrile is a fraud, but try telling that to someone who went to Mexico, got it, and now has no cancer.

Doctors say the so-called youth shots given in Switzerland are a joke, but try telling that to Millie, who is 76 years old and looks about 50. For 15 years she's been going once a year to Switzerland for her perk-up shot. She's married to a man nine years younger than herself, and he looks ready for a wheelchair. But Millie has blond hair and smooth skin, and she dances up a storm while her younger husband sits around trying to catch his breath.

Just what is reality? You might think you would never perform a homosexual act, but what if someone held a gun to your daughter's head and threatened to pull the trigger if you wouldn't? That would change your reality pretty quickly.

Many Americans were disgusted when Vietnamese people stranded on an island began eating each other to survive. The reality is: in their situation eating human meat wouldn't be difficult at all. It's been done many times, so it can't be that tough. You eat a big brown-eyed sweet innocent cow, don't you? You won't mind having its left leg for dinner tonight. Being stranded on an island could give you the emotional charge needed to feel as passive about a dead buddy's body. Why not give life to life, rather than let a person rot?

What is really real, instead of what you think is real, or what somebody told you is real? Is God real? They don't call Him that in China, or in India. And who are they? Are "they" really real? Start testing your own reality. It may be different than you think.

I invariably test reality with clients who think their particular problem is earth-shattering, as I did with Eva, a divorced mother whose boyfriend had just dumped for for a younger single woman with no children. After she gave me the bit about her life being ruined because she'd lost the one she loved, I asked her, "Do you really have a problem?"

Yes, of course she did. She'd lost the only man she ever truly loved.

"But is that really a problem? What if you don't do anything about it. Then what will happen?"

Nothing would happen.

"Then you don't really have a problem, do

you? You're creating a problem, but you don't have one. That's the reality. Your lifetime is no more in the scheme of things than a quick flick of a flashlight on and off, and you're telling me your life is ruined because your boyfriend dumped you? You gotta be kidding me. With six billion people running around the face of the earth, you're getting yourself all upset because this one jerk who obviously doesn't recognize a winner—if you are a winner—dumps you and probably did you a favor by getting himself out of your life? The reality is—what's the difference? When you haven't even checked out Washington and Arizona and Nebraska yet, you're telling me this guy is the key to the kingdom?''

Eva's sobs continued. She was into a prize-winning crying jag.

''Tell me what would happen if you got a phone call right now. You've already paid 40 bucks for your session with me, you've been here three minutes, and you get a phone call telling you your kid just got hit by a truck and he's on the way to the hospital. What would happen?''

She held back her tears. She'd leave and go to the hospital, of course.

''But what about all this heart-wrenching misery you're into? What about that?''

Well, that would have to wait. Her kid is more important.

''Yeah, I understand that. But why did your kid have to get run over by a truck for you to figure that out? Why did you have to have a real tragedy for you to figure out that what you're into really isn't that important, that many things you could think of right away would immediately take precedence over this earth-shattering experience of getting dumped by your boyfriend. If the building was on fire, what would you do then?''

We'd have to leave, of course.

''Would you cry all the way down 11 flights of stairs?''

Well, no. She'd be busy just getting down the stairs, trying to get out of the building.

''Oh, then the reality is that what you're into, what you seem to think is such a ball buster, is really not that big of a deal, is it? Because we could think of 15 things in a big hurry that would change this feeling-sorry-for-yourself trip. Why do they have to happen for you to realize that? Why do they have to happen for you to realize that some jerk who ditched you is not worth the total emotional investment you're giving him by turning the break-up into a total disaster?''

Try testing your own reality. If you're honest with yourself, you'll admit that your reality, caused by the accidents of your life, continues to be reality because you haven't chosen to change it. The choice of reality is yours.

People have a hard time adjusting to the fact that they have a choice. They feel emotionally handicapped, as if they have no right to make a choice. Most people react to most occurrences as if the choice has already been made for them because they have no emotional programming that tells them, ''Stop! First of all, I have a choice.''

Try to ingrain two classic catch phrases into your subconscious. ''I have a choice'' should become your automatic first thought in every situation, and ''That's your choice'' should become an automatic second thought when another is involved in something affecting your life.

Just because someone seems to have made a choice for you does not make it so. Tell yourself, "That's another person's choice, and that's okay unless it affects me—and then it becomes my choice as to what I'm going to do about it."

It's your choice if you want to sit and cry, and that's okay if you want to do it. But I don't care to cry with you, and that's my choice. The freedom of choice is a terrific principle: I have mine, and you have yours. I don't choose yours, and you don't choose mine.

Take a lady all dressed up waiting to go out for an evening on the town with her husband. When her husband comes home staggering drunk, she gets upset, unhappy, frustrated, and angry because he's ruined her entire evening by his choice to get drunk. Most women in such a situation assume their choice has been made for them. The reaction is: "Look what you've done to my evening, you bum. Look how terrible, how crummy I feel. We can't go out now. The evening is spoiled."

Most women forget they have a choice. The husband has made his choice by getting himself too drunk to do anything but sleep it off on the sofa, but the woman can make her own choice. She can put her intellect to work to think of options for the evening by asking, "What am I going to do to salvage the evening and deal with this particular problem? I'll obviously have to scratch the original plan because that won't work, but I have a choice. I could throw a screaming fit and really give him hell, trying to hurt his feelings like he hurts mine all the time. I could pack my bags, go to a motel, and file for a separation or a divorce tomorrow. Or I could get drunk myself so I won't even care that he's an inconsiderate slob and that I'd like to slap his snoring, sneering face. Or I could go out to dinner by myself and take in that monster movie that's been getting rave reviews. Or cuddle up with the latest best seller that's been gathering dust on the coffee table for the past two weeks. Or I could cook up something with Mary, whose husband is out of town, or call my single friend, Sandy, who may not have a date for tonight. Or I could call George and get together with him because he's always understanding and warm and comforting when Fred and I are having trouble."

That's where psychofusion comes in. After intellectually choosing the most attractive option, she needs the feeling to go with it. Right now she feels crummy because her husband's choice to get drunk gave her that feeling. The subconscious came up with a feeling for the situation, but she doesn't have to keep the feeling she got by accident. She can choose to change that feeling by going inside a memory and retrieving the feeling she needs.

She can remember the last time she and George went to a football game when Fred chose to spoil another evening's original plan. She was able to deal with her frustration because she had somewhere to go and someone to be with. It was pleasant—stopping for a couple of drinks after the game before she came back home and found Fred still conked out on the sofa, the TV blasting. She was able to handle her anger then.

She can go inside that memory and get the

feeling she needs to act upon her choice of how to salvage the evening. If the memory doesn't provide the right feeling, she can go to another. Whatever she needs is in her subconscious if she will only bother to retrieve it. She doesn't have to settle for the first feeling that happened to surface.

The key to psychofusion is a recognition of where you're at, an awareness that you're into a downer that you can choose to get out of. You can choose to re-live feelings of pet memories vivid enough for you to visualize and pop into your head on command. Go back to certain memories that inherently have specific emotions that you can identify and feel again.

Most people deal fresh and new with just about each problem they're confronted with, predicated on negative emotional reactions. As a result they have less basis to deal with it successfully because they treat the problem with brand new feelings and knowledge, as opposed to relating it to past feelings and knowledge. No problem is new. It involves a different place, different people, and different circumstances, but it has the same feeling.

Once you learn to find the feeling, the emotional charge you need, you can change your reality. If you don't have the subconscious programming to give you the feeling you need, you'll have to go get it with new experiences. You can find it.

Even though you haven't realized it up to now, you find feelings to fuse to your intellect all the time. When you're bored, aggravated, or tired, you call a friend to meet you for lunch. What's the purpose? You don't like the feeling you have, so you arrange something that you know will be pleasurable. You need a particular feeling, so you go get it. You change the reality of being bored, aggravated, and tired.

You can change any reality you choose to change. Whenever you're confronted with something you don't like, tell yourself, "Wait a minute here! I don't like this. I'm going to put my intellect to work figuring out how to get out of this situation because I've got a choice."

Then step outside and observe the situation clearly and decide what kind of feeling or charge you need to change the reality of the situation. Take a deep breath, say "melt and relax," and visualize a time when you had the feeling you want. That's the way to break in the new reality you've chosen for yourself.

**INSTANT RECALL:** "Who's doing what to whom—really?"

# CHAPTER 11

# Preparing for Change

BEFORE CHANGING YOUR life for the better, you must be both emotionally and intellectually prepared. Being intellectually prepared means more than intellectually knowing you want the change. It means being intellectually capable of handling the change once you have it. If either the emotional or intellectual preparation is missing, a change can be for the worse instead of the better.

Amelia wanted a change, but she was channeling her intellectual desire in a disastrous direction. A 23-year-old overweight but pretty Mexican, Amelia had tried time and time again to commit suicide. She obviously hadn't tried very seriously because she hadn't succeeded, but even while seeing one psychiatrist after another, she continued making feeble attempts to kill herself.

In my office she leaned back in the reclining

chair and began her pat story. She'd told the story 5,000 times by now, so she had it all memorized, and she got into her act. Because her mother and father were divorced when she was three years old, she never had a father. When she was 17, she married a man 10 years older for the security he represented. He worked in an automobile factory, made a good salary, and had all the benefits of medical insurance that paid her psychiatrists' bills.

Amelia had two kids right off the bat, and she felt they tied her down and were controlling her life. She felt gypped, ripped off, cheated, because she hadn't had time to grow up. She'd never had a life of her own.

She had started punching her 5-year-old and 3-year-old around. She didn't want to hit them, but she was so frustrated she couldn't help herself. Her husband had little to do with her. When he was home, he just played with the kids and watched television. She was super negative, depressed all the time. All she wanted to do was kill herself.

Amelia's emotional charge to change her life wasn't properly fused with her intellect. She had an emotional charge to change her life, but in a misguided way. The only way she knew to change the reality of a life she didn't like was to leave it.

"If you want to kill yourself, that's okay," I told her. "But it's stupid because it's not going to accomplish what you want it to accomplish. You want people to feel bad when you're gone. You want to get even with your husband and your kids for keeping you from having an opportunity to grow up, and you want to sacrifice your body so they'll miss you when you're gone. For openers, three days after you're under the ground, they won't have time to worry about you. You're under the ground—who cares? If you really want to get even with them, let's get on with it and 'get' them."

Amelia warmed up to this approach. The psychiatrists had tried to plug in their goody-goody-two-shoes philosophy to this lady who didn't want it. Telling her she was lucky to have two healthy kids and a loving husband who supported her well wouldn't cut it. Intellectually she already knew that, but it didn't change the reality that she was miserable with those kids and that husband. She could tell herself all day that she was lucky, but if she didn't feel lucky inside, it didn't make it so.

"Do you want me to help you?" I asked. "Do you want me to help you get even with these people?"

She did.

"Okay, but you've got to promise me one thing. If you want to kill yourself, that's great. But if you're going to do it, just cancel any appointment you have with me. Don't screw up my life just because you want to kill yourself because I can give that appointment time to somebody else. Is that fair?"

She was pretty shocked, but she agreed.

"Let's take what you've got," I said. "You hate. You want to get even with your husband. If you really want to get even with him, get yourself happy, get attractive, get your act together, feel good about yourself, and that'll just kill him. It'll kill him because he isn't that way. He'll eat his heart out because you've got all the things he wants. You really want to hurt him—that's what you do. Don't kill yourself—that's stupid. He'd win then. He's trying to kill you emotionally now, the way he treats you.

"Get a job, and get out of that house. Begin to lose weight. You could look good if you wanted to. You're looking bad because you're trying to get even with everybody, but that isn't working. It's obviously not working because you're depressed as hell, and you want to kill yourself. Also, you've got to plan and arrange to dump your husband because you don't love him and you never did. So we're not going to try to get you to love him. Don't worry about it. Let's blow him off. But let's do it intelligently. Don't be an asshole about it. Plan it so he's okay, so he can function, and your kids can function."

Amelia's dark Mexican eyes grew rounder as I talked to her, but she was getting into it. "Do you think it's okay for a woman to leave her children?" she asked. She went into a long harangue about how she hated the way she was punching her kids around and how her husband was a good guy who would see that they were well taken care of.

So I said, "Yeah, it's okay. There's nothing wrong with your leaving your kids. First of all, they're going to be there six days or six months from now. If you want to go back, you can. Secondly, you're not helping the kids by being there. You're ruining both of them, so staying with them is no big sacrifice. You told me your husband is a good guy, an honest guy, a loving guy, a good father. If all that's true—great! Leave the kids in that atmosphere totally. Don't give them a little love when he comes home and then total bad news when he's gone. Do you think that's good for the kids?"

Amelia repeated that she felt she had never had

a chance to grow up. She couldn't reach down inside herself and retrieve that feeling she needed because it wasn't there.

"Fine," I said. "You don't have that feeling, right? Go get it. Do your own thing. Give yourself a chance to grow up."

Amelia weighed 195 pounds on her first visit. When she came back six weeks later, she was down to 175. She had a job as a truck driver, the kind of job that made her feel good. She had been locked into a little house, and now she had the freedom to travel around in something big and safe. She and her husband had talked to their priest about separation, which was imminent. She had a plan, a way of changing her life, and she was emotionally charged to do it.

The hate she felt wasn't there anymore. It wasn't necessary anymore because she no longer wanted to hurt anybody else. The negative became a positive, and it's entirely possible Amelia will return to her husband and children after she's had a chance to feel that she's grown up. If she does, it will be because she chose to, and it will be on her terms.

With psychofusion she prepared herself emotionally for a positive life change and fused her emotional charge with an intelligent decision to change her life.

Because being intellectually capable of handling the change is vital, I always ask my clients about their intellectual preparation for the change they want. I asked this question of George, who wanted to open his own restaurant but was afraid to do so.

George was a dynamic, go-go guy who had managed several restaurants for other people. He wanted to own his own place and be his own boss. When I asked if he had done his homework and was intellectually capable of handling a restaurant, he told me he had the necessary financing and expertise.

"I know how to run a restaurant," he assured me. "I can do it standing on my head. I'm just afraid to try it."

With hypnosis I took him back to a time in his life when he had no fear of undertaking a new task, took the feeling from that previous time and fused it with his intellectual desire to own his own restaurant. I told him he was ready, that he was tired of being a hired hand. It wasn't necessary for him to work for someone else because he had matured to the point he was able to take everything he'd learned and put it into his own restaurant. He was ready to be his own man, and there was no need to be afraid. Instead, he could have the feeling he'd had before when he didn't fear new undertakings. George used psychofusion and auto-echo regularly to maintain his feeling of confidence.

Within a month he opened a restaurant in what appeared to be a good location. After the restaurant had been open for five weeks, I went there for a meal.

"This pork chop is lousy," I told him. "The potatoes are cold and undercooked. The tossed salad is soggy."

George said I was being too particular.

"I'm the only one sitting in this joint eating," I said. "Doesn't that tell you anything? The food is crummy."

He wouldn't admit it. He wouldn't admit he

had any reason to worry about his business succeeding.

The fact is: George couldn't intellectually handle what he said he could handle. Everything he'd learned wasn't enough for him to be a successful restaurateur. A piece of him was a self-destruct mechanism that forced him to bury himself. He went straight down the tube. An Arthur Treacher's that opened at the same location is making money hand over fist.

Maybe his failure will be a good lesson to him. Maybe he needed the experience of bankruptcy programmed into his computer so he would know what it feels like and be able to avoid it next time around. Maybe if he psychs up the courage to try again, he'll intellectually realize he needs something beyond his own abilities to succeed, like a cook who knows how to prepare pork chops, potatoes, and salad.

Let George's experience be a lesson to you. Don't psych yourself to write a novel if you've never written a short story. Don't psych yourself to enter a Mrs. America contest if you weigh 195 pounds. Don't try building your own house if you've never built a storage shed. Don't enter the Boston Marathon if the farthest you've ever run is to the mailbox and back.

Fuse the feeling you need with your intellectual desire for change, but be sure you've done your homework. Be sure you can handle the change —physically, emotionally, and intellectually.

**INSTANT RECALL:** "Learn before you leap."

# CHAPTER 12

# Tackling Your Fears

MOST PEOPLE FILL their lives with shoulda, coulda, woulda's. Dan shoulda taken a job in Saudi Arabia way back when it was offered to him. He coulda taken it because he was single then and didn't have to answer to anybody. He woulda taken it except he was afraid his invalid grandmother would die while he was out of the country for two years, and as her favorite grandchild, he felt compelled to be around for her final days.

Shoulda, coulda, woulda's are generally followed by "still wanta's." Twenty years later Dan still wantsta take a job in a foreign country, but he no longer shoulda (and risk job security at age 39?) or coulda (and take along a wife and three children to a lower standard of living and poorer schools?). But if he shoulda, and coulda, he certainly woulda.

Yeah, sure. Believe Dan's story, and you'd believe the earth is flat and icebergs exist in Brazil. The fact is when a person has a shoulda, coulda, woulda story, he needs an emotional ass-kicking to get him rolling with something he still wantsta do. He needs to forget the rationalizing rigmarole about why he can't prod himself to action. He needs to accept that he's afraid. Unfortunately, the fear is way back in his subconscious. Instead of being afraid to do something he shoulda, he ought to be scared to death not to. Fear, which keeps him confined to the accidents of his life, prevents him from doing the shoulda's he needs to change those accidents to choices.

Anytime you have a problem, it's because you're afraid of something. You're afraid to confront the problem, to deal with it, to accept the consequences, to face the possibility of failing. Fear is every problem's bottom line, and you can't be afraid to start at the bottom if you want to solve your problems.

Fears are learned. You're born with zero, not a single one. A baby has reactions, such as to loud noises and sudden movements, but he has no fears until they get programmed into him with his initial childhood programming. Whatever fears get planted in his subconscious stay there to control his life unless he confronts them and resolves the problems they're causing.

A classic fear instilled into children is a fear of strangers. Some people have trouble getting into cocktail party chatter 40 years later because they've been programmed to avoid relationships with people they don't know. If you're one of them, accept that you need to improve your childhood attitude and understand that other people—even strangers—need you.

Just saying "hello" to someone is an ego stroke that makes him feel good. Everyone likes acknowledgment of his existence. You have value to other people because you can give them this good feeling, and if you don't do it, you're being unkind. If you do fulfill their need, you're maturing. It's valuable for you to outgrow that childhood pattern because you'll get to know more people, and you'll be more comfortable with social activities.

You can mature a childhood fear of strangers, and then replace it with new programming after confronting the fear. So you talked to the woman in line behind you at the bank today. You admired her sweater and commiserated with her about the building's excessive air conditioning. She didn't offer you a piece of candy and try to entice you into a car. Your brief encounter with her put programming into your computer that says all strangers can't be bad. You can selectively reject the programming that kept you shy and withdrawn if you repeat this positive experience enough.

If you're afraid of horses, you confront that fear by patting a horse on the nose. Didn't kill you, did it? You work up the nerve to let the horse eat a carrot from your hand. Not as bad as you thought. Even brushing his mane doesn't take a CIA agent's nerve, as you'd suspected. Continue confronting that fear, and you'll find yourself mounting the horse to go riding before long. If he throws you, so what? You survived the ordeal,

didn't you? You won't be as afraid next time you
have an occasion to ride.

You know what riding a horse feels like now.
Your subconscious has new programming to override the old programming that kept you afraid.
You didn't have the feeling you wanted—being comfortable with a horse—so you went out
and got it. You didn't settle for the feeling your
subconscious gave you by accident.

Whatever fears you now have, you must get new
programming or retrieve positive memories to
overcome them. If I ask you to meet me at a well
known restaurant in a familiar part of your city,
you'll drive there at the appointed time without
giving it a second thought. If I ask you to meet me
at a restaurant you've never heard of, in an unfamiliar section of town, you'll intellectually
figure out how to get there, but it'll be a major
production.

You'll have to find the address and look it up on
the map, or call the restaurant and ask for directions. You'll allow yourself extra time because
you'll be afraid you might get lost. You have that
fear because you have no source to go back to for
directions to that restaurant. The next time you
meet me there, it'll be no big deal. You've been
there. You've had that experience. You can do it
again.

Fear can't control you if you have sources to go
back to. Bob Hope says he's scared every time he
does a show. Intellectually he knows he has no
reason to be afraid, but emotionally he can't help
it. He's able to overcome his fear because he has
hundreds of sources in his experiential base telling

him he can confront it. He confronts it every time he goes on stage, and he's always a smash as a stand-up comedian.

Myra was afraid to go out with men because she was born with a congenital hip deformity that caused her to limp. A clean, angelic-looking 28-year-old, she wanted to be attractive and sexually active, but was afraid to accept a date.

"You look terrific," I told her. "You're friendly, you're nice, you've got pretty blue eyes, nice blonde hair. You've got everything you need to be attractive to men. Instead of worrying about what's wrong with you, all we're going to worry about is what's right with you. I don't even want to hear what's wrong with you. What's wrong is over and done. That's ancient history."

But Myra wanted to talk about her deformity. She remembered when boys asked her for dates as a teenager, her parents would ask, "But where can you go? If there are stairs, you'll have problems. What can you do?"

She bought the program and turned down the dates, allowing her parents to keep her a cripple and an obedient child. Even at age 28, she went to church with them every Sunday, just as she'd done since she was a kid.

Now, even though a fellow at the office had asked her out a few times, she couldn't bring herself to accept his invitation. We had to find the emotional charge strong enough to reprogram her emotional computer that convinced her she'd mess up if she accepted a date.

Under hypnosis, her subconscious gave us the answer. She talked about the feelings she had when this fellow asked her for a date, the fear that she might embarrass him with her funny walking. She talked about knowing that her parents wouldn't like her leaving the house with a man they didn't know—or any man, for that matter.

I asked her, "What would make it possible for you to go out with him? Tell me what could happen that would make it okay?"

Her subconscious didn't even hesitate. "If *I* asked him, that would be different because he wouldn't go unless he wanted to." Obviously, he would not ask her if he didn't want to either, but the subconscious is not always logical. Feelings often lack rationality.

"Did you ever think about that?" I asked. "Did you ever think about asking him out?"

No, she never did.

"You didn't think about it, but you felt about it, or you wouldn't have been able to tell me," I said. "You've never intellectualized it, but you've had that emotional desire. You're telling me if circumstances were a little different, dating would be okay. Well, make it different then. Change it. You ask him for a date."

After the hypnotic session, we plotted her method of approaching the young man.

"If you had two tickets to the Fisher Theatre, you'd need two people to use them wouldn't you? Could you ask him to go with you to see a play? Are you willing to do that to see what happens and to see how it feels?"

She was, but she was scared. I bought two tickets to force a commitment from her, and with hypnosis I reinforced that she was a mature, attractive, adult woman with the emotional courage to extend an invitation to a man. She played the tape of the hypnotic suggestion for several days, rehearsing emotionally until she felt capable of asking the man out. At last she did it, he accepted, and they dated for several months. Although they broke up, her hip deformity no longer kept her from dating men. She had overcome her fear, and the last I heard of her she had moved out of her parent's home and was engaged to be married.

Arlene was a bundle of nerves when she walked into my office. A recent widow, she was afraid to live alone. For the past 30 years of her marriage, she and her husband had worked side by side together, and he never went any place without her. When he died, she moved in immediately with her sister, who quickly tired of Arlene's possessiveness. Arlene was so terrified of being alone that she wouldn't even let her sister go shopping without her. Arlene couldn't go anyplace alone herself because she didn't know how to drive. Naturally, she was afraid to learn how.

"What are you afraid of?" I asked her. "The worst that could happen to you is that you could die, and you might as well be dead anyway as to live your life in constant fear. When you're afraid, you're regressing to a childhood fear of being alone, and that fear made sense when you were five years old and needed your mom and dad to take care of you. But you can take care of yourself now. Even though you were with your husband all the time, he didn't take care of you the way your fear is making you think. You worked side by side with him. You contributed. You were capable, so why are you afraid to be capable now?"

Arlene said she felt unable to function without her husband.

"But you *are* functioning, aren't you? You're still eating your meals and staying alive, and you're functioning. You just have to decide what kind of reality you want to function in. How small is the box that you're willing to live your life in? Because as long as you're afraid, the perimeter of your circle of reality is mighty small. Your fear is the perimeter of your existence. That's as far as you can go. If you attack that fear, then it expands what you're boxed in to. You have to practice the attitude of being afraid to be afraid, or you're going to be boxed in forever.

"What would your husband want you to do— become a basket case now that he's dead? Wouldn't he think that all his efforts and companionship with you were a total waste of time because once they're lost, you're too weak and too insecure to be your own woman the way you were when he was alive? Wouldn't he prefer that you continue on and do what you need to do to have a good life?"

Arlene learned to use psychofusion to get the feeling she needed to enjoy life, the feeling she lacked without her husband. She went inside herself and got the feeling of her husband being there. She let him be with her in spirit. When she worked the crossword puzzle, as they used to do together, she assumed the emotional attitude and the feeling of a day well done, the way it had been after they shared their late dinner together. When she showered, she began singing as she shampooed, just as if he were in the adjoining bedroom listening.

After her son-in-law invited her to go disco dancing, she started expanding her circle of reality outside her own home, taking her husband along in spirit. She became a vivacious smiling terpsichorean conquering a new choreography instead of a wallflower afraid to even fox-trot. Before long she enrolled in a driver's training class. Once she realized that the worst that could happen was that she would die—and she realized that she didn't fear death—fearing life became irrational to her. Only then was she able to do what she should do and wanted to do.

If fear dominates your life, you could spend the rest of it telling self-pitying shoulda, coulda, woulda stories, still wanting the emotional fulfillment you'll never get. You can feel sorry for yourself if you like—that's your choice. But I won't feel sorry for you—that's my choice. You can't expect to succeed if you're afraid to start at the bottom, tackling the fears that restrain you.

**INSTANT RECALL:** "Freedom from fear begins right here."

# CHAPTER 13

# Flooding Your Fears Away

IF YOU'RE A rational person, you don't want to live boxed in by an irrational fear. Don't start fighting tigers, or jumping off precipices, or darting across an expressway in bumper-to-bumper traffic. Very little brain power is needed to distinguish between an irrational and a rational fear. Once you've determined that yours is irrational, just do whatever it is you're afraid of doing, and you will conquer it. Psychologists call this technique flooding. Once you flood yourself with experiences that prove the fear is irrational, what's left to be afraid of?

Irrational fears don't make any sense, so why get nervous over them? You didn't pick your fears—whatever they are—so don't take them personally. Some programming in your subconscious put your fears into you, but you can get rid of

them. You can either get new programming that
will override the old, or improve the childhood
perception of something that made you afraid.

Even if you can't isolate a specific incident that
put fear in your subconscious, you can eliminate
the fear anyway. You don't need to know why you
have it. Lynn knew her fear of blood had existed
since childhood, but she didn't know why. She remembered when other children played doctor and
nurse, she didn't want to participate. Although
there was no real blood in make-believe, the blood
existed in her mind, and she wanted no part of it.

When other young girls had ambitions to be
nurses, Lynn dreamed of being a teacher. When
every other girl in her college sorority donated to
the Red Cross blood drive, Lynn refused.

For all those years Lynn surrendered to her fear
because she had no reason not to. If she went to a
movie with gory scenes, she simply closed her eyes
when she anticipated something bloody, telling
her husband to let her know when she could watch
again. She missed more than half of the movie
*M.A.S.H.*, never watched medical programs on
television, and saw the movie *Alien* without ever
daring to look at the creature itself.

She did nothing about her fear until she became
pregnant. Then she realized her child might get a
bloody nose or a cut knee, and she shouldn't wait
until then to find out what her reaction would be.

"You've got to start on the basis that your fear
doesn't make any sense," I told her. "Other
people look at blood all the time, and nothing
happens to them. Are other people stronger than
you are? Have they got some quality in them that
makes them more capable of handling the sight of

blood, some immunity that accidently got passed
out to them, but didn't get passed out to you?

"What's the worst that could happen if you
looked at blood? First time, you might faint—
that's the worst. And you can have your husband
with you, and he'll revive you right away, so that's
not a bad penalty if it happens. Probably that's
not going to happen, but even if it does, what's the
odds of it happening again?

"If you faint that first time, you'll realize when
you wake up that the fainting didn't make sense
either. The blood didn't do anything to hurt you.
It just lay there, being red. There's nothing bad
about blood because you sure wouldn't be alive to
be afraid if you didn't have any of it.

"If you decide to take a look at blood, what's
the best that could happen? You could start enjoying movies and television more, that's for sure.
When you dish out $4.50 for the cinema, you
won't need to keep your eyes closed during $2
worth of the action. And you could be certain that
once you've seen enough blood without going into
the screaming meemies or dissolving into some
eighteenth century damsel in distress act—you can
be certain you'll be capable of taking care of a cut
finger when you need to."

The solution is always so simple. Confront the
fear—that's all you have to do. Lynn simply
opened her eyes. The first time she sweated
profusely, but what's a little perspiration? The
second time she clenched her hands so hard she
had fingernail indentations on her knuckles. She
kept flooding herself with looking-at-blood experiences until she had enough new programming
to override whatever the original programming

was that made her afraid. She still didn't like what she saw, but she wasn't afraid to see it.

Sometimes when a person is irrationally afraid, confronting the fear all at once is emotionally impossible for him. If you're afraid of elevators, you don't start conquering your fear by riding in a crowded elevator to the twenty-fifth floor. It makes more sense to take along a friend, wait for an empty elevator, and ride up one floor. Next time get on an elevator with another person, and ride up two floors. Keep working at it until you've worked yourself up to a crowded elevator going to the top floor.

The procedure takes time, but desensitization works. Just keep working yourself deeper and deeper into the most frightening aspects of your irrational fear until it is reprogrammed. Eventually your subconscious says to itself, "I've had enough experiences on elevators now to know there's nothing to be afraid of." You have then reprogrammed your subconscious to feel the way you want it to feel instead of the way it happened by accident.

Before taking the first step, you can use psychofusion to help yourself. Pick a specific memory when you were not afraid. Say "melt and relax" and get inside that memory. Relive it. Bring the same feeling of confidence that you felt then into your present situation.

You can also use psychofusion to imagine yourself in the situation that you fear. Before getting on the elevator to ride one floor with your friend, visualize yourself doing it. If your hands get clammy and your heart starts racing, say "melt and relax" and visualize it again. Keep putting that imaginary scene in your mind until you get used to it. This mental behavioral-rehearsal technique can help give you the nerve to ask your boss for a raise, the spunk to demand good service from an inconsiderate clerk, and the courage to express an unpopular opinion at a dinner party. Ridding yourself of fears can change your life.

Any time a person fails to make a change he wants in his life, fear is the reason—usually fear of failure. People have a hard time accepting the concept that there is no such thing as failure. Absolutely not. There are only degrees of success. Some of the degrees of success are not so hot, but they have value, and you learn from them. You grow. If you refuse to make a life change you want because of fear of failure, you stagnate. You get stuck with those accidents you didn't pick but are afraid to change.

Steve wanted to change his life, but he was afraid to leave the security blanket of a big corporation. With his factory job he had a steady paycheck, union protection, excellent benefits, and he didn't have to work very hard. However, he was bored out of his skull. Although he wanted to sell real estate, he had only half-assed dedication to his dream. He sporadically took courses in real estate, but even after qualifying to enter the business, he was afraid of betting on himself.

When you're struggling with a decision about a life change, ask yourself two basic questions: What if I do it? and What if I don't do it?

"What if you do it?" I asked Steve. "You'd have an opportunity to get rich, you'd be independent, you'd be your own boss, and you'd be happy because you wouldn't have to punch a factory timeclock any more and be bored eight hours a day. But what if you don't do it? You'll never know how good you could be if you don't try it, you'll always be living from paycheck to paycheck, and you'll be a shop rat the rest of your life."

But what if he did it and failed?

"If you do it and fail, you never look at it as a failure. You look at it simply as an education and an opportunity to grow. You're only 25 years old, so you'll have ample opportunity to start over if you fail. But to talk about what happens if you fail is stupid. You're not going to fail. You're good-looking, bright, and you have all the pieces. You've got the education you need. You may not succeed quite as much as you'd like, but you're not going to fail because you have the capability of doing what it is you say you want to do."

Steve used negative psychofusion to give him the emotional nudge he needed. When he was not at work, he went into his memory and saw himself standing on the assembly line, slapping fenders on cars. He heard the blasting bedlam of the factory, smelled the dirt and grease, and felt his own clammy perspiration. He visualized himself growing old on the line, still slapping on the same fenders and still bored out of his gourd. He'd been there. He'd had that experience for seven years. He tried to get inside that feeling and became scared to anticipate having it for another thirty-seven years. He practiced building an aversion to that feeling and then flashing to a time when he had confidence in himself and felt so much happier.

As an extra motivation to help him overcome

his fear of leaving his security, he bought a new house and a new car, putting pressure on himself to make more money to meet the payments comfortably. Each time I saw him I'd add to the negative programming he was building toward his job with scornful comments. "How do you like being a shop rat?" I'd ask. "Do you like it, shop rat? You picked it, you know. That's your choice. Is that where you're at? Is that your whole program? Is that as far as you can go in life?"

Steve finally became afraid to be afraid. Only then could he take a chance on himself. Three weeks after he quit his job and started in real estate, he made a $4,500 commission on a sale. His first year in the business he made $44,000, and he expects to make more than $60,000 this year.

You too can do what you want to do if you can only overcome your fear of trying. If you don't have the education you need, go get it. If you can't afford the tuition, make the money for it. If you don't have the maturity you need, pay whatever dues you need to grow into whatever you need to become. You must flood yourself with whatever experiences you need to eliminate fear from your life before you can flood your life with fulfillment.

**INSTANT RECALL:** "Fear must go for me to grow."

# CHAPTER 14

# Turning Distress into "Blisstress"

STRESS IS A KILLER. Research indicates that emotional stress contributes to high blood pressure, gastrointestinal problems, and a variety of illnesses.

Stress makes gastric juices damage the stomach's fragile lining, contributing to the development of ulcers. Stress causes blood pressure to soar, leading to strokes and heart attacks.

Stress sends many to the liquor cabinet, the divorce court, and the unemployment office. It makes people unhappy and causes them to die before their time.

Stress happens when anything that feels like a pain, strain or goes against your grain prepares your body to do battle, but unconsciously battles your body.

In spite of extensive research by doctors and psychologists, little is known about why certain stressors devastate one person and have little effect on another. The rigors of an air traffic controller's job can cause hypertension in one controller while having no marked effect on another. The trauma of getting a divorce may be viewed with extreme distress by one person but accepted as a tremendous relief by another.

Obviously, the stressor is not the reason for stress. Stress is the unconscious emotional reaction that the stressor creates within an individual. When you suffer stress, it's because the 90 percent of you that's emotional is controlling the 10 percent of you that's intellectual by spouting out an emotion that you didn't pick and don't want, an emotion that can make you physically ill.

You can psych yourself out of stress by choosing emotions that turn "distress" into "blisstress." Anything that arouses emotion is a form of stress, but you can choose a pleasure form of stress: blisstress. Because the entire range of human emotions is slumbering within you, you can resurrect your best feelings and reject the negative feelings that battle both your body and mind. You can use psychofusion to become a person who refuses to let stressors make your life unpleasant.

First, you must recognize that you are under stress. Quickly sense that a pressure or emotional disruption is rising within you. When your airplane is delayed indefinitely because of an icy runway, ask yourself, "What good is it going to do for me to become upset?" When you get billed $300 more than your lawyer estimated as the fee for your last will and testament, ask yourself, "Is my rage going to change the bill?"

Be aware that you are unconsciously choosing

to feel angry or frustrated. Be aware that you can choose to feel a positive, productive, controlled attitude in these situations, as you can in any other.

Use psychofusion. Breath deeply. Inhale deeply to flood your body with oxygen. Exhale slowly as you think "melt and relax" to instruct your body to release any feeling you do not want. You can feel immediate inner control if you allow yourself to do it.

Recall a specific feeling you've had before—one that would eliminate your stress if you had it now. You've already drawn upon feelings of relaxation that you have stored in your subconscious. Visualize the memory now, vividly in your mind. Go inside the memory and let the feelings flood back into your mind and body.

Act with those feelings to overcome your stress. Re-experience the positive feelings by flashing the memory picture in your mind and going inside the memory to retrieve its emotional benefit.

Don't take the stress personally. The runway did not become icy as a personal vendetta against you. The lawyer did not underestimate his fee and then overcharge because he thought you were a soft touch too insecure to question the discrepancy. Disassociate from the stress by purposefully stepping outside of yourself and observing the stress, rather than becoming caught up with its unpleasant experience.

Analyze what is reaching inside to make you feel the way you do. Recognize that it's an unconscious emotion that you didn't choose. Go back to the memory of relaxation that you did choose, and enjoy the memory. Dwell on it, and make it come true.

If the feeling of distress is still trying to dominate your emotions, close your eyes, relax, and mentally repeat the following sentence ten times, pressing a finger or thumb with each repetition: "Good feelings are my choice." Through auto-echo this idea can be programmed into your subconscious until your subconscious accepts it as true.

Although you can learn to eliminate stress when it occurs, your best bet is to lessen its opportunities for happening to you. You can do this by analyzing specific things that make you stressful and reprogramming your attitude toward these particular things. Like fears, most stressors are irrational, and recognizing them as such will help you eliminate them from your life.

Edna was under stress because her husband had had a heart attack. Although doctors assured Jim he was making good progress and could work his way back to a normal life with the proper exercise and medication, Edna felt it was her duty to worry herself sick about the possibility of his dying.

If Jim so much as decided to hammer a nail in the wall to hang a picture, Edna mother-henned him to be careful. She fussed and fretted about every meal she prepared, making a daily ordeal out of choosing low-cholesterol food and mastering new fat-free recipes. She was worrying herself so sick that she was steering herself toward an earlier death than her husband's.

"I wouldn't be a good wife if I didn't worry," Edna said. Only after she was able to accept that she was choosing her stress was she able to eliminate it.

Edna's stress is a common one. Many people worry because they feel they wouldn't be good people if they didn't. What kind of a mother wouldn't become a nervous wreck if her kid skipped school, sassed the teachers, and refused to crack a book? What kind of a daughter wouldn't become depressed if her elderly mother became senile? That kind of rationale makes misery run rampant.

Accept that becoming upset in any situation accomplishes nothing. No person in your life has a right to obligate you to upset your own.

Another common attitude that leads to stress is the feeling that if things don't go exactly right, then they must be considered bad. If a hostess drops the platter of white fish at her dinner party, she assumes the whole evening is a flop. If a secretary gets reprimanded for a typing error, her whole day is ruined.

Why choose such a negative attitude when you can assume a positive one? Always tell yourself that no day is bad. It's just that some are better than others. Start evaluating the bad things that cause stress in your life, remembering that there is no bad—only varying degrees of good.

If you believe that happiness is impossible unless you are loved and appreciated by virtually everyone, you belong to the substantial society of self-ass-kickers. If you believe that you must be competent in everything you undertake, you've got a perfection compulsion that will continually frustrate you. Nobody can be loved and appreciated by everyone. Nobody can be perfect. It's too bad, but it's a fact, and if these two hang-ups cause you stress, it's because you've chosen unrealistic goals and unconsciously chosen to feel bad when you can't achieve them.

Other common beliefs that cause stress are the

convictions that happiness and unhappiness are caused externally, and that one's past history determines one's present behavior. Forget them both. You know by now that you can reach inside yourself and retrieve any emotion you choose—no matter what your environmental circumstances are—and you can reject negative programming that caused your past history, programming your future the way you want.

Experts who have studied stress recognize that exercise and relaxation techniques are helpful in warding off stress. If you undertake an exercise program, be certain you choose one that you can enjoy on a regular basis. If it becomes hard work and drudgery, you're certain to abandon it and feel guilty, resulting in even more stress.

A simple relaxation exercise done when you feel stressful and before you go to bed at night can be very helpful. Follow these directions: Lie down on your back in bed, and let your feet separate as they naturally tend to do. If your feet are held together with your toes straight up, you're tense. If your arms are folded over your chest or your hands clenched together over your stomach, you're tense. Let your arms drop to your sides with the palms of your hands up. Now you're in a proper position to relax.

Concentrate on nothing except the particular part of your body that you ask to tense and untense. You will ask each part of your body to tense itself, hold the tenseness for five seconds, and then slowly untense itself. As the tension is leaving, focus your attention on the sensation of it disappearing from your body.

As you begin, tense your right leg and foot, pushing your heel away and drawing your toes toward you and holding for five counts. Then, untense—but don't release all the tension immediately. Concentrate on releasing it slowly, focusing your mind on your leg as it releases, all the way to the tips of your toes.

Tense your left leg and foot, pushing your heel away, drawing your toes toward you for five counts, and gradually untensing, letting the tension drain from your knee, down your calf, out of your ankle, out of your heel and your instep, and all the way down to the ends of your toes. Your legs should feel heavy with the tension all released.

Concentrate on your pelvic area. Draw in your stomach, tense your buttocks, and hold for five counts, and slowly release, feeling your buttocks loosen and your stomach lift back to position as you concentrate only on that part of your body.

Concentrate on your chest area. Move your shoulders back toward each other, tensing the back and the rib muscles for five counts. Release, slowly allowing the tension to work its way out of your back, your shoulders, your neck, and your chest, concentrating on those parts of your body as the tension disappears, leaving your torso limp like a rag doll.

Tense your arms, down from your shoulders and all the way into your clenched hands for five counts, and release, slowly letting the tension drain from your upper arm, your elbow, all the way down to your wrist and your hands and the tips of your fingers as you open your hands with the palms up.

Tense your neck by leaning your head backward for five counts. Untense, concentrating on the tension draining out of your neck, and your spine, and even your buttocks as you continue to relax.

Concentrate on your face. Clench your jaw and mouth, raising your cheeks, tightening your eye-lids and wrinkling your brow. Pretend you're making a childish angry face and then release, allowing your chin to lower, your lips to part slightly, your cheeks to drop, and your brow to smooth out its wrinkles.

Your body should now feel that it is sinking into the mattress as you force your mind to check each part of your body to see if it is completely relaxed. First your right foot, your left foot, your right leg, your left leg, your buttocks, your stomach, your chest, your back, your shoulders, right arm, left arm, your hands, your neck, your chin, your mouth, your cheeks, your eyes, and your fore-head.

As you're completely relaxed, let your mind visualize a happy relaxed memory, get inside the memory, and re-live it.

You'll find that practicing this relaxation exer-cise not only will relieve stress when it occurs, it will also give you extra energy during the day and help you relax at night when you're having trouble going to sleep.

By combining psychofusion to choose the emotion you need to counteract the stress you didn't choose, auto-echo to program the good emotion in your subconscious, and this toe-to-head relaxation exercise—you can turn distress into "blisstress." When stress threatens to do battle with your body and mind, you can be the victor.

**INSTANT RECALL:** "Good feelings are *my* choice."

# CHAPTER 15

# Developing Self-Love

LOVE IS THE highest, best emotion humans can experience, but like all emotions, it dies if it isn't practiced. Even if you've not had a loving thought toward another human being for the past 20 years, you still have the ability to love. The emotion is there in your subconscious, lying dormant because something in your subconscious chose to spout out hate, or fear, or self-pity, or resentment, or jealousy, or some other less desirable emotion that smothered and suppressed the love emotion.

If you can't love others, it's a sure bet no one can love you—not even yourself. If you try to love someone else when you don't love yourself, you're looking for a vicarious justification for your existence and trying to create a dependency upon someone who can provide for you what you can't provide for yourself—your own self-esteem.

It won't work. It's artificial. It's a fake. You might temporarily gain someone's affection, but that affection won't last. If you don't like yourself, you perpetuate that self-deprecating image, and even those who try to love you will eventually recognize that you're a loser. They will decide that *you* know you better than *they* know you, and if you dislike yourself, why shouldn't they?

People need love. A child reared without affection will be a screwed-up adult. An adult who claims he doesn't need other people is generally a person afraid to take the risks of loving. Loving opens you up to be hurt because the persons you love might not love you back. It's like walking a tightrope. You have a chance of getting hurt every minute you're on it, but you've also got a chance of experiencing the sublime. However, that risk doesn't exist when you're practicing self-love, a prerequisite to developing a love relationship with anyone else.

You're born with the recognition that you are Number One, but that feeling is quickly programmed out of your subconscious. You learn as a child that loving yourself is wrong. Love others—that's society's rule. Don't be selfish. Don't be proud. Don't be greedy. Don't be conceited. An addendum that doesn't get programmed is the qualification that selfishness, pride, greed, and conceit are bad traits only if they interfere with other people's rights to their own selfishness, pride, greed, and conceit. Used positively, these emotions can make you a better person—a person who can love himself and thus have the ability to love others.

If you are selfish about the way you look, you

take good care of your body.

You take the time to follow a daily exercise routine. If you are selfish about the way you look, you'll learn to love your own appearance—because you'll look good. It's a vital step toward loving your complete self.

Georgina was in the typical captured-by-the-husband-and-children shell before she lost 40 pounds. She changed her cooking habits over her children's protests and even got a job over her husband's protests. Her children survived without their usual fresh-from-the-oven treats after school, and her husband treated her with new respect after her salary actually exceeded his.

She called me about nine months following a hypnotherapy session in which we concentrated on training her to love herself. "I just want to thank you for giving me permission to be myself," she said. Of course, she gave herself the permission. She just needed an outside source to confirm that it was okay for her to be selfish about the way she looked, proud of the capabilities she had, greedy about using them outside her home, and conceited about her accomplishments. She couldn't be herself until she could first love herself.

If you're an average programmed-to-be-selfless individual, you probably cringe at the idea of Georgina becoming conceited about the change she made in her life. Of course, you feel that way. When you got programmed with a list of good and bad feelings, conceit led the list of no-no's.

By definition, conceit is "an exaggerated opinion of oneself and one's merits." Have you ever stopped to consider what our world might be like if we hadn't had people with exaggerated opinions of themselves and their merits? Most progress came because someone—in spite of society's scorn—invented the light bulb, the telephone, the automobile, and the airplane. In the scope of existent knowledge at the time, those people certainly had exaggerated opinions of themselves, didn't they?

Abraham Lincoln is considered one of our greatest presidents, but few people remember that out of 11 times he ran for office, he was defeated nine times. How many of his contemporaries, who voted him down for dog catcher and county clerk, thought he had an exaggerated opinion of himself to run for the presidency? He kept believing in himself when few others idid. He hung in there; he didn't quit. If that's conceit, who can criticize it?

People are similarly programmed to believe pride is bad. A woman giving a dinner party may sweat over a hot range for hours preparing delicacies to serve her guests, but when the compliments come, she feels guilty about accepting them with pride. "It was nothing," she'll say, or "I can't take the credit; it's my mother's recipe." or "My cooking can't begin to compare with Martha's, or Jennifer's, or Jane's." Show me a woman who answers, "Yes, it is delicious, isn't it?" and I'll show you one who recognizes pride as a necessary ingredient of self-love and loving others.

Forget the adage, "Pride cometh before a fall," and coin your own catch phrase, "Without pride, there's no love at all."

If you can't take pride in yourself, you're putting your heart out to be stomped on if you try to develop a love relationship, and the same is true of being greedy.

Forget all those hackneyed definitions that profess true love to be selflessness, putting another person's pleasure before your own. That's heavy-duty heartbreak. If your self-love is strong enough and reality-oriented, then a combined love with another can share the same strength and reality. If your self-love is strong, you feed, nurture, develop, and double your feelings by sharing them, but if you don't love yourself, you have nothing to give that will grow, allow intimacy, and stand the test of time.

You must learn to be greedy. If you're the giver, and the object of your love is the taker, the so-called love you have will become a farce. Such situations exist in many marriages, especially those consummated in or before the 1950s. Women then, who were programmed to believe that their husband's desires should always come first, are tangled in a tug rope, with one end pulling them to be liberated from servant status and the other telling them that's where they belong.

Their husbands are not the culprits. After all, they were programmed the same way, to believe a wife's duty is to serve her husband's interests. The dilemma created a species of superwomen, who held down two full-time jobs—one in the home and one outside. It also created resentments that destroyed loves that once existed. Marriages that survive with love intact are ones in which each partner has enough self-love to allow the other the privileges of selfishness, pride, greed, and conceit.

Develop those qualities within yourself, and you'll find yourself loving other people and being loved, but it won't happen overnight. Except for couples going through the first throes of romance—with the stomach butterflies, the starry eyes, and the can't-live-without-each-other convictions—the love emotion has to be practiced. The initial love crazies that physically and mentally afflict you don't last unless they're consciously practiced on a regular basis.

You can't establish a love relationship with someone and expect it will stay the same for 20 years. If it does, you don't really have love, you have a rut. Otherwise, each person in the relationship would have grown, matured, and changed, and their love would have grown, matured, and changed with it. The secret to perpetuating the love is having growth, maturity, and change that are acceptable to both parties. Then, although bells no longer ring when a kiss is exchanged, the love can be a comfortable one. Like an old shoe, it still feels good, even when it has lost its initial allure.

Like all emotions, love is a feel, not a think. Like all emotions, self-love and the ability to love others rest within your subconscious, and you can retrieve the feelings. Think back to a specific occasion when your love for someone was so strong it virtually overflowed from your body. Remember the excitement. Remember the fear of losing it. Remember the this-is-all-that-matters emotion that pushed everything else from your mind.

Breathe deeply, think "melt and relax," and bring that emotion to the conscious level. Awaken it within yourself. Bring it up time and time again, looking upon the psychofusion exercise the same way you look upon painting. If you want a durable, shiny surface on a table top, you spread the paint lightly the first time. After it dries, you add another thin layer. You keep putting on layers until it's thick enough to please you. You can rejuvenate the love emotion the same way, layer by layer until it's durable and shiny. If you get it in gobs, it won't last.

Don't make the mistake of thinking love is forever. Inevitable changes are not always emotionally acceptable to both parties in a love relationship. Because you once loved someone doesn't mean you'll always love that person. That would be like Thomas Edison discovering the light bulb and saying, "Okay, the job is done." If that had happened, we'd still be squinting through hazy, yellow light. The first light bulb wasn't good enough. It needed refinement and development. Why should our emotions be any different?

Believe me, if any spark of love still exists between you and another person, you can retrieve all the emotions that originally went with it if you want them. When I do a hypnosis demonstration, I generally select one couple as the lucky couple of the night. After hypnotizing them both, I give them the suggestion that they will have an evening of perfect, uninhibited lovemaking, along with further elaborations. Follow-up phone calls and letters from couples I've selected have indicated some heartening results, such as the thanks from a woman who got pregnant that particular night after three years of trying. Only once have I received a complaint.

Malcolm came to see me a week after he and his

wife had been the lucky couple. He complained that he couldn't eat, couldn't sleep, couldn't do his work, or pay attention to anything.

"Have you ever felt this way before?" I asked.

He had. He could remember feeling that way when he was 17 years old.

"What happened then to make you feel that way?" I asked.

That's when he met his wife. She had affected him that way. He lost his appetite, his concentration, his entire composure.

I laughed. "Do you know what's happened to you?" I asked. "You're back in love again, just like when you were a teenager. When I zapped you and Tish as the lucky couple, I must have told you you'd love her just as much as you did when you first fell in love. And that's exactly what happened. You've got the lovesick crazies for your wife."

Under hypnosis, I modified his teenage love trip so he could eat and sleep and work. Remember Malcolm when you think it would be just super to love like that first initial love. Some love symptoms would be best left in your subconscious to be remembered fondly, not to be relived.

Let only the best in you come out. Don't be afraid to love your good points, to flaunt them, to let them be a visible part of you. Don't accept your negative points as aspects of yourself that make you unworthy of self-love. If you don't like them, bury them. Acknowledge their existence, and then let them die through neglect. Reject the emotions that remind you of your flaws.

Don't try to love somebody else until you've learned to love yourself. It's impossible to go outside yourself and create an emotion that's not happening on the inside. Then you'd be trying to pull something from the outside to the inside, and that doesn't work. You can only project a love feeling from within, where it's waiting for you to find it and make it live again.

**INSTANT RECALL:** "I love becoming me."

# PART THREE

# Breaking
# Bad Habits

# CHAPTER 16

# Understanding
# Why You Eat Too Much

VERY FEW PEOPLE eat because they're hungry.
Most of my overweight clients tell me they've
never felt hunger because they always eat before
their bodies reach that stage. Many feel most of
the time as if they've swallowed a self-inflated
basketball.

Why, then, are most Americans overweight?
Simply because we're programmed to believe that
no matter what the problem, food will make us
feel better.

Let's face it—eating is a pleasure. It's a primal
gratification; it feels good. It's also a natural
tranquilizer that calms you down. An ice cream
cone will make you feel better when its sugar gets
into your bloodstream and gives you a temporary
"high." A cup of hot chocolate will warm you up

when you're chilled from shoveling snow off your driveway.

The oral gratification of eating is plugged into us before we can even think, especially our addiction to sugar. If a baby cries, he gets a pacifier dipped in honey. If a toddler behaves, he gets an ice cream cone. If he doesn't cry when the doctor gives him a shot, he gets a lollipop. If he's celebrating a birthday, he gets a big cake. If he eats all the spinach and other lousy vegetables, he gets dessert.

Eating is a token of love that amplifies the pleasure of a sharing experience. When you visit a friend, the first thing he or she does is offer you something to eat or drink. If you refuse you're rejecting not only the food or drink, but his or her hospitality.

You learned that lesson years ago when Mom cooked your favorite dish as a token of her love for you. If you happened to be full and didn't want to eat it, she was insulted. You got the message quickly. You're programmed to believe if you don't eat what people offer you, you're a bad person because your refusal will hurt them.

Americans are also programmed to eat more often than necessary. The traditional three square meals a day is a capitalism rule, not a human rule. Companies sell a lot more food if people eat three times rather than twice a day, as is customary in many countries. Capitalism also contributes to the American early dinner hour. If you eat dinner at 5:30 p.m., you'll be hungry for chips, popcorn, pretzels, or other munchies before you go to bed. If Americans were programmed to have dinner at 8 p.m., the way most Europeans do, company

profits would drop. People would be in bed before
the cookie craving caused a raid on the pantry,
and Orville Reddenbacker would be back on the
farm.

With hypnotherapy I've helped thousands of
clients reprogram the emotional computer banks
that keep them captive in the kitchen. If you can
change the way your mind feels about food, you
can lose weight without getting a thyroid trans-
plant from a tapeworm or having your tongue
stitched to the top of your mouth. Change your
mind to change your life, and you can change your
body. It's that simple.

You can do it yourself. You can psych yourself
slim. You psyched yourself into the fatter body
you're carrying around now. Some of you men
deliberately started gaining weight as teenagers
because you wanted to be macho. In your mind at
that time, bigness represented masculinity. You
didn't realize then that once you started ac-
cumulating those extra pounds on your body,
you'd eventually stretch it beyond the sex appeal
stage.

Some women put on weight deliberately for exactly the opposite reason. Being sexy wasn't comfortable. Remember the first girls in junior high to
start developing bustlines? They felt weird. The
majority of their friends were still flatchested, and
they didn't like being different. Their classmates
made fun of them, and they got catcalls about
their bra lines showing through their sweaters.
Some were also teased by fathers who made a big
issue about their babies blossoming into woman-
hood. A little extra weight made that embarrass-
ing bosom a little less noticeable. A lot of extra

weight could almost hide it completely.

Such people as these psyched themselves into changing their bodies. Later when they wished they had their old, thin bodies back, they continued following their excessive eating patterns even though they knew they shouldn't. Even though they intellectually wanted to change, they were emotionally arrested.

Some people start overeating when something new puts unfamiliar pressures on them. George and his wife Gloria came to me to lose weight after four years of marriage. Neither had a weight problem before they became man and wife, but after four years George was 55 pounds overweight, and Gloria needed to take off 40.

George was an old-fashioned guy who felt a wife's place was in the home. Because Gloria was unstimulated by her typing pool job, she readily quit to stay home. Her big task every day became preparing dinner. She devoted herself to studying cookbooks and experimenting with fancy recipes calling for rich sauces, sour cream, and made-from-scratch pasta. In cooking she found the creativity lacking when she sat all day at a typewriter. Cooking became her job and her biggest contribution to their marriage. Very efficient at this occupation, she had dinner on the table when George walked through the door at night.

George felt he had to eat whatever Gloria cooked because if he didn't, she became upset and depressed. Why mess up their relationship over a meal? he reasoned. His program was to eat heartily every night to satisfy his wife's emotional need to feel that her creativity in the kitchen was appreciated.

When they discussed their eating habits with me, Gloria said she cooked because she thought George expected it of her. She was surprised when he told her that elaborate cooking wasn't necessary to satisfy him and make him feel she was a good wife.

As single people, they had no weight problems because they ate only when hungry. To lose weight, their life change was cutting out dinner because neither was hungry at that time. They ate because the clock said it was time. In making a life change to lose weight, Gloria turned her creative urge to macramé, and the five-course feasts became a thing of the past. Instead, they had late soup or salad suppers when their stomachs said they were hungry.

Some people start overeating because of lack of sexual gratification, either physically or emotionally. If you're not getting physical or emotional gratification, the next best gratification is food. Like with sex, eating has a climax: you swallow. Many sexually active women don't have climaxes during intercourse. They reach a certain high sexually, and they're left hanging because there's no ending, no resolution of their feelings. The gratification they didn't get in bed the night before, they'll try to get the next morning by eating. They'll raid the kitchen thinking, "I've got a craving for something, but I don't know what it is." The chocolate candy bar didn't quite quell their desire, and the cheese didn't do it either. They never quite get that craving they equate with hunger satisfied because it's not food they really need.

Some people overeat because of sleeplessness.

Lying in bed with their minds still going in passing gear while trying to shift their bodies into low, they subconsciously remember the little snack and glass of milk that Mom used to give them before bedtime. Whatever they raid from the refrigerator to overcome insomnia stays like a lump in their stomachs until breakfast, which increases the lump.

Few people are immune to the excessive calorie intake caused by America's favorite passive pastime, television watching. Television hypnotizes: that's why calling it the Big Eye is most appropriate. Commercials are programmed to cause an emotional arousal in the watcher, often combining arousals geared toward food and sex.

When you see dimples of frost running down a pop bottle, you feel thirsty. When you see a pretty girl grinning after eating a chocolate bar, you feel envious. Your subconscious tells you that you could probably get that happy, satisfied feeling with something just as good to eat. Remember, your subconscious feels; it doesn't think.

Brian's subconscious habitually told him to eat in the middle of the night when he was sound asleep. He would walk to the refrigerator, fix a snack and almost finish eating it before he awakened. As this pattern continued night after night, he became more and more upset at the extra calories he was putting into his body. Although he was tall and skinny, he was horrified at the thought of gaining a single pound.

Brian put a padlock on his kitchen door, hoping he'd wake up before he got it unlocked and completed his nightly ritual. Sometimes he awakened while unlocking the padlock, but other times he didn't.

When he came to me for help, I reprogrammed his subconscious to go back to a memory of eating something he enjoyed and eat it in his sleep whenever he had a night-time craving. After that, instead of satisfying his craving in the kitchen, he satisfied it in his dreams. Other clients have used this memory-of-something-tasty technique while awake.

Cravings occur for many reasons, and few people can avoid the food cravings caused by drugs. People have a cocktail or a glass of wine before dinner to whet their appetites, but if you're trying to lose weight, you don't need either. Some drinkers can't understand why they're overweight because their food intake is minimal, but they don't realize they're drinking 1,500 calories a day. That's all the average woman should eat just to maintain her weight. To lose, she's got to eat less. The average man won't lose a pound if he consumes 2,000 calories a day, so he can't afford to have 1,500 of those in liquor. Although smoking pot doesn't add calories, it gives people the famous "mad munchies." Day-old socks would taste good after a joint.

Many people eat because they haven't learned to handle an emotional conflict, and they swallow or chew their problems. Judy started gaining weight when her husband began working the night shift, leaving at 3:30 p.m. After Judy put the children to bed, she spent the evening with her old pals—bags of chips and bottles of Coca Cola. She worked her way up to 24 bottles of coke a day, with around 150 calories each. Every day she took the carton of empty bottles back to the store and replenished her supply for the lonely night ahead, when she put 4,000 excess calories in her body.

No wonder her weight zoomed past the 200 mark, and her marriage started floundering. Her hard-working husband, who had 100 pounds more of a wife than he'd bargained for when he married her, no longer found her attractive to come home to after midnight. Judy lost weight only after dealing with her loneliness and filling lonely evenings with college correspondence courses, which came in handy after the marriage broke up.

Eating can be a primary defense mechanism. When you go to a party where most guests are strangers, what's the first thing you do? Probably you head for the buffet and get something in your hand—either an hors d'oeuvre or a drink. Either one gives you immediate oral gratification, the same security you felt when the bottle was stuck in your mouth at age six months.

Very few people gain weight because they're too dumb to know any better. Your "thinker" doesn't eat; your "feeler" eats. All the logical, rational, intelligent thoughts you have will not do a thing to help you lose weight. That's why you can gobble down a dozen cookies and give yourself hell at the same time. You are saying to yourself, "I've got to go on a diet, and eating all these cookies is dumb," but you keep shoving them down anyway.

The part of you that feels doesn't care what you think. That's why it's easy to get red-hot excited about losing weight right after you've had dinner. The savage has been soothed, and you feel ready to tackle that new diet in the latest *Family Circle*.

Four hours later, when the beast is grumbling for a snack, you're not nearly so charged with the idea.

If you eat too much, you must recognize it's because of some subconscious programming that emotionally pushes you to food. It's that old 90 percent of you beating out the 10 percent that knows you need to diet.

You must face facts: you can't fight or beat the emotional part of your mind, because it's too strong. The only solution is to convert it. You must convert the strength of your emotions in the direction you want because the subconscious is like a raging river that cannot be stopped—only rechanneled.

**INSTANT RECALL:** "Swallowing my feelings will make me fat."

# CHAPTER 17

# Choosing to
# Lose Weight

WHETHER YOU'RE 10, 20, or 100 pounds overweight, you've probably tried to take off those excessive pounds by dieting. That's how most people
try to lose weight, but they've got it backward.
Dieters go after their protruding stomachs and
flabby arms instead of the insecurities, loneliness,
boredom, or frustration that causes them to eat
too much. They try to attack the body when it's
the mind that's misshaped the body.

Your body is a product of your life, and you
need a life change—not a body change. Nothing
else will work for permanent change.

Dieting, for instance. The first three letters of
"diet" are D-I-E. That fact in itself is not a turn-
on for most people. No one goes on a diet because
it's fun. A diet gives you guidelines to lower your
calorie intake, but a diet doesn't change your at-

titude. A diet is a repression. It doesn't keep you from wanting to eat ice cream, cake, or candy. You still crave those things, but your diet puts you in a little box that makes ice cream, cake, or candy off-limits—but only temporarily. People don't stay on diets forever. A diet does not make a permanent attitude change or a permanent eating pattern change. That's why dieters are always on a yo-yo syndrome—up and down, up and down. They know that losing weight is easy. It's keeping it off that's murder.

When you go on a diet, you get angry right away. You're mad because you can't eat certain things like a normal person. You hope you lose weight quickly so you can eat "normally" again. You're in an emotionally imposed prison, but you know you're going to get out some day. When you get out, you're going to go right back to where you were before, gobbling down goodies and loving it.

Take Weight Watchers. As a Weight Watcher you are trained to eat three to six times a day. You get turned into a life-long food machine whose job is to eat particular foods that cause your food budget to zoom. Eating becomes the big event of your day, and you spend hours planning and preparing what goes into your mouth.

Weight Watchers teaches you to satisfy the childlike primal gratification, while psyching yourself into new adult attitudes eliminates food as a primal gratification. Don't let anyone kid you. The only permanent slenderizing way to eat large quantities is to chew everything, but swallow nothing. Best wishes to anyone who wants to try.

Some fat people get desperate enough to have their mouths wired to lose weight. That's like putting a muzzle on a mad dog. He still wants to bite, but he can't as long as the muzzle is on. Take it off, and that's a different story. The weeks of repression lead to oral revenge.

Short of amputation, an intestinal bypass is the only guaranteed way to lose weight, but one out of seven people die when they get it. The operation bypasses 18 to 22 feet of your small intestine so you can't digest food. Food doesn't stay in your stomach long enough to get into your body. A bypass short-circuits a person's metabolism. People who have had bypasses need to take B-12 shots and liquid vitamins because the body can't absorb their food's vitamins, which are eliminated from the body too quickly to be absorbed.

One client came to me four years after having an intestinal bypass. When she had the operation, she weighed 320, and four years later she weighed 270. On a 5'3'' female, what's the difference? You couldn't see she'd lost those 50 pounds. She lost more by reprogramming her emotional computer bank that made her eat her problems away instead of growing up to solve them.

To reprogram yourself, you must choose to lose weight. You may think you've already done that, but your choice lacks the proper charge, or those pounds wouldn't still be a problem.

Betsy, a 25-year-old, didn't have a strong enough charge to keep her from crunching munchies while watching endless hours of television. She was unhappy, but her depression wasn't reason enough for her to choose to lose weight. Depression is not as strong as fear, or embarrassment or anger. It's not traumatic. It's not immediate. She didn't suddenly get lonely or suddenly get depressed. The feeling came upon her gradually, but steadily, as she continued to eat her way out of the social scene.

At work one day when her slimmer co-workers were selecting a restaurant for dinner that evening, a handsome young man said, "Ask Betsy. Fat people always know the best places to eat."

The comment added insult to injury. Not only was Betsy, as usual, being excluded from the evening's plans, she was being ridiculed for her body. The comment forced Betsy to make a spontaneous choice based on her unconscious reaction to it. In her case the choice was good: she chose to change her body so she'd never hear a cruel comment like that again.

She came to my weight clinic one time, and I didn't see her again for another three months when she came back for reinforcement. Before the session started, she asked, "Do you remember me?"

I usually remember all my clients, but her face wasn't familiar at all.

"I was in your weight clinic three months ago, and I've lost 55 pounds so far," she told me.

No wonder I didn't recognize her. She'd lost the equivalent of a small child from her previously over-plump body. She looked terrific. I asked her how she liked being thin.

"My life's great," she said. "I used to stay home all the time, but I've got a social life now. I can wear pretty clothes now, I've taken dancing lessons, and I've had a job promotion. Couldn't be better."

Betsy's unconscious reaction to an unkind comment changed her life, but she was lucky. An unconscious reaction can be negative. The same comment made to another person could confirm the fact that the person's a fat loser who's never going to change. It could cause a person to choose to continue abusing his body. As it did for Betsy, an insult from somebody you respect can spur you to succeed in changing your body. But unless you accept the insult as a challenge to change, you can let an insult nail your negative feelings about yourself into your subconscious even stronger.

You've got the choice. Next time someone insults you with a look or a word, let the insult spark you to spurn sugar instead of sending you to the box of chocolates. Accept the insult as the emotional charge you need to make a positive life change.

Make the choice to let your body be a billboard. Remember that if you don't lose weight, you will have limited social mobility. Only a certain number of people are interested in fat girls or fat guys. You have to either accept that, or decide you don't like it and do something about it.

Unfortunately you even have to be suspicious of your friends' reasons for liking you. Many insecure, good-looking people like to have fat friends tag along with them because the contrast makes them feel better. They know that by comparison, they look super.

If you remain fat, you will always have certain physical limitations. How many 250 pounders do you see racing down a ski slope? Not too many. How many ballet dancers who weigh in at 180? Not a bunch.

The fact is: you're going to look ridiculous doing certain things, such as water skiing or ice skating. You'll probably avoid fast dancing because you don't want all your body parts flopping around. You'll look weird instead of sophisticated when you cross your legs, if you can cross them at all. You'll have to continue contending with those looks that say, "nice face, bad body" along with the comparisons you know are always made between you and slimmer persons.

Accept the fact that if a friend sets you up with a blind date, the friend is obligated to tell the other person you're fat. Otherwise, the blind date will be bummed out when he sees you. Your friend will have to go to the "She's-got-a-great-personality" line because the "dynamite body" bit doesn't fit.

When anyone describes you to anyone else, your weight has got to be mentioned. Let's face it, a 20-pound roll hanging over your belt isn't exactly sexy. People don't get particularly excited about somebody with three chins.

The reality is that fat is a physical turn-off. When you meet anybody, right off the bat you make an emotional judgment of that person based on his physical presentation. If a guy picks you up for a date in a Volkswagon with a fender flapping, he makes a totally different impression from the guy who arrives in a Mark V. Forget the quality of the guy. You make an immediate judgment by what he drives, what he wears, how he looks. People who deny this are fooling themselves.

The popular cliche, "You can't tell a book by its cover" is simply a sham. The adage that "Beauty is only skin deep" is a lot of baloney too. Fat is only skin deep too, and so is skinny. Maybe you truly believe "It's what's inside that counts," but try running up to every person you meet, grabbing him by the lapels, shaking him, and saying, "I'm really a nice, clean sweet person inside. Don't let my body fool you." Good luck.

If you went to the race track, would you bet on a fat horse? It would be pretty tough to do, wouldn't it? You'd want to bet on the lean, sleek one.

Because personnel managers are the same way about people, accepted generalizations about fat people—whether they're right or wrong—result in limited job opportunities for overweight people.

First, fat people are considered lazy because if they weren't so lazy they wouldn't be fat. Second, they're considered dumb. It's impossible to look bright and intelligent when you're 80 pounds overweight. Third, fat people are considered unclean because "fat" and "pig" go together, and pigs are dirty. Fourth, employers assume if you're sloppy with your own body, you'll be sloppy with their company's product.

Some employer assumptions are pretty reasonable. Fat people die early, so why invest in somebody who's got an extra 50 pounds his heart has to pump blood through? Why invest in someone whose odds are high for having a heart attack and getting arthritis? Why take the liability for problems associated with being fat when a skinny person is available for the same job?

You use the same kind of logic as these employers. If you went to a doctor for help in losing weight, would you stick around if the doctor weighed 280 pounds? No way. You'd forget how smart he is, how many degrees he earned, and how successful he's been with his medical practice. Your emotions would turn you right off and send you searching for a skinny doctor whom you'd trust to do his job.

Maybe your job is the reason you're overweight. If you don't like your job, coffee break is a big event, and lunch is the highlight of your day. When you get home from a job you don't like, you feel you deserve a little goody as a reward for your suffering all day. If you live to be 100 years old, you sleep eight hours a day—that's 33 years. If you work eight hours a day at a job you don't like, that's another 33 years. That's 66 years of nothing.

If you're going to lose weight, you need to either quit that job or change the job procedure so that it becomes pleasant to you. You need to make a life change, before you can make your body change.

You've got to realize that whatever reasons you've had to lose weight up to now haven't worked. So quit kidding yourself. Dump them. Find the emotional charge you need to keep yourself away from calories. Find something strong enough to make you consider asking a friend to hide your refrigerator. Find a reason that can constantly drive you to succeed on a day-to-day basis until you get the goal you want.

**INSTANT RECALL:** "My body is a billboard."

# CHAPTER 18

# Finding a Motivator
# for Slenderness

THE BIGGEST REASON people can't lose weight is because they don't have a reason to. If you don't pay your income tax, Uncle Sam will come after you. If you don't make your house payment, you'll be living in the street. If you don't make your car payment, you'll be on the shoe leather express. But if you don't lose weight, what's going to happen? There's no immediate penalty.

To reprogram yourself to choose to lose weight, you must find an emotionally charged reason to do so. Ask yourself: What happens if I *do* lose the weight? (that's your positive motivator—your payoff) and What happens if I do *not* lose the weight? (that's your negative motivator). Either a positive or a negative motivator will work if it's strong enough.

Your motivation must be a stomach-flutter,

gut-grabber turn-on that can get you excited or afraid. Otherwise, it won't be forceful enough to provide the daily reinforcement you need as you develop new attitudes toward food. Because you will no longer be getting the immediate gratification of food, your subconscious must equate the eventual payoff with an ultimate worth-while gratification.

What kind of emotionally charged reason will work? A class reunion coming up, or a wedding where you'll see people you'd like to impress, or a sudden sexual desire for a particular person— these can be great motivators.

If you're single, wanting to be attractive to appeal to the opposite sex isn't enough. It sounds good, but it doesn't work. If you want that kind of motivation, pick out a particular person. If you're female, pick a fellow who's handsome, desirable, and unquestionably too suave to be attracted to anyone with a body like yours. Start savoring this fellow. Psych yourself to want him, knowing the only way you can possibly get him is to get your body in shape. He's your payoff. Winning his attention is reason for denying yourself the immediate gratification of food.

Wanting to keep a spouse's love isn't strong enough reason to lose weight either. A woman who weighs 115 pounds when she gets married may think it doesn't matter if she puts on a few extra pounds while she's confined to her home caring for her babies. If she feels locked in, not expecting to go anywhere or be anyone other than a Mrs. to her Mr., her problem is in her life, not her body. She can keep eating until her body becomes a turn-off to her husband. That extra 40 or 60 or

80 pounds he didn't marry wipes out the visual stimulation she used to give him, and he can lose interest in a hurry. The same goes for a woman if her husband gains too much weight. Nevertheless, wanting to rekindle a marriage's dying embers generally isn't spark enough to cause a person to lose weight. Discovering that your husband or wife is sleeping with someone else—might be.

Reasons that people think will work often don't carry an emotional charge strong enough to make them succeed. For instance, many clients come to me because their doctors have referred them, to lose weight. They'll be healthier if they lose weight and they know it. Their doctors didn't need to tell them that. But wanting to lose weight to improve your health isn't a strong enough reason, not unless you hurt bad enough from the excess weight or unless by some quirk the weight is guaranteed to kill you, and you aren't ready to die.

Others tell me they want to wear nicer clothes. I ask them, "If you could wear better clothes, where would you wear them? Where would you go?" Most don't have an answer to that question, and that's why clothes as a motivator to lose weight won't work. The life change—the specific reason they have a strong emotional urge to wear nicer clothes—has got to come before the body change. They need a positive charge.

Your positive charge might sound negative, and you must weigh its validity on the basis of what it accomplishes for you—not for anyone else. Ralph, an auto-factory worker, wanted to lose weight to dump his wife and his assembly line job. However, he didn't want to dump his wife unless he had a chance of finding another, and with his appearance, his options were slim. After losing 117 pounds, he could put two of himself into the pants he used to wear. He looked great, and his new appearance gave him confidence. He divorced his wife, quit his job, opened his own party store, and remarried. He found his positive motivator.

Before you begin your plan to change your mind to change your body, take the time—no matter how much time it takes—to verbalize and visualize your positive motivator to make the change. Being able to visualize your motivator to lose weight is vital because you will be using this visualization with the psychofusion technique.

If better health is your motivator, ask yourself: Do you hurt bad enough to care? If you don't, find another motivator.

If more energy is your motivator, what would you do with the extra energy that you can't do now? Is visualizing yourself doing these things enough incentive to keep you away from food?

If self-respect is your motivator, ask yourself: Is your body the only thing about yourself that you do not respect? Will losing weight truly give you the self respect you want, or does your life need other changes too?

If your motivator is to look younger, why? How is looking younger going to change your life? If your motivator is to have a better sex life, why? Is sex important enough for you to change your lifestyle for it?

Would a money pay-off curb your appetite? If cash could be your positive motivator, set up such an incentive. If you don't have a wife or a husband to offer you a suitable reward, set aside a certain cash sum each week. Plan to let it accumulate for a particular splurge that you will not allow yourself until you reach your goal.

Would a vacation do the trick? Would a travel escape cut down on your food escape? Or would a new job be the solution—an opportunity for a career and extra money?

Is there a particular sport you want to pursue? Are you willing to pay the price to play that particular game?

Only you can determine your own positive motivator. You must find it! In the world of choices open to you, some incentive in this vast world must be strong enough to spur you toward the life change you want.

If you absolutely cannot find a positive charge, you'll have to settle for a negative charge. Give a thousand dollars to a friend, and commit yourself to losing three pounds a week. The first week you don't lose three pounds, the friend gets to keep the thousand dollars. That turns you off to a thousand dollar Dairy Queen in a hurry. It might even entice you to eat only with your feet, maybe even with your shoes on.

Set up a commitment so painful you can't avoid succeeding. Look for the feeling that will make you go at it. Be like a jockey or a model who must either keep their weight down or lose their jobs. Find the feeling that will make you a person who has no choice but to lose weight, and make a commitment to be that person.

Okay, you've found the feeling. You have intellectually decided upon a feeling that's strong enough to give you the daily emotional charge you need to stay away from food. It is a feeling that you can visualize. You can go to it in your mind and see the feeling. But you know that intellectually deciding upon a feeling is not enough. You've got to fuse that feeling into your emotions with psychofusion.

Start by breathing in deeply, exhaling slowly, and thinking the words, "melt and relax," telling your body to cooperate. Close your eyes, and visualize your feeling—your motivator—in your mind. Let the feeling flow into your mind and body.

Put words to your feeling. State your motivator in one short sentence. While letting the feeling you chose flow into your body, repeat that sentence ten times, pressing a finger or thumb with each repetition. You're using auto-echo to emotionalize your feeling and make your emotional subconscious mind agree with your intellectual conscious mind. You're getting all the parts of your mind working together to help you achieve your goal.

You must take the time to do this psychofusion and auto-echo exercise daily. Repeat it any time you feel tempted to overeat, even without taking the time to get yourself into complete relaxation. If you're tempted to indulge in strawberry shortcake, move each finger and thumb slightly, thinking your emotional charge with each movement. You will be surprised how easily the urge disappears. You'll no longer need a choke chain on your neck with a leash attached to keep you from opening your mouth and stuffing it.

**INSTANT RECALL:** "Lay-off for pay-off."

# CHAPTER 19

# Reprogramming
# Old Eating Attitudes

ONCE YOU'VE FOUND a motivator strong enough to make you lose weight, you'll be surprised how easily you can reprogram old eating attitudes.

First, you should be making the psychofusion and auto-echo techniques daily habits. On a regular basis you should be letting the feeling you need flood into your body to keep you aimed toward your weight loss goal. You should have repeated the sentence describing your motivator hundreds of times as you plug it into your subconscious with auto-echo. Only then is it time to start plugging in new eating attitudes with the auto-echo finger pressing technique.

Certain catch phrases can easily be implanted into the subconscious. Try a new one each week, starting with "Proper food feels the best."

Remember, your subconscious is programmed

to believe that ice cream feels better than spinach and candy feels better than fruit. Your "feeler," not your "thinker," is what eats. You've already got your "thinker" on your side in the battle against calories, and an emotionalization of the idea that proper food feels best will get your "feeler" in agreement with your goal.

Another easily emotionalized catch phrase is "Junk food is my enemy." Repeat it often with ten finger or thumb presses, and your subconscious will eventually accept this statement as true. You'll know you've successfully reprogrammed the attitude that leads you to popcorn, potato chips, and pretzels when the word "enemy" pops in your mind when you see them.

"Fat body—fat head" is a catch phrase that works to keep most people from overeating. No one likes to feel stupid, and once the subconscious accepts the idea that an overfed body symbolizes an under-nourished brain, it won't be so turned on to devouring three wedges of pumpkin pie.

"Leave a little—lose a little" is a catch phrase that will eventually eliminate all guilt feelings you have about leaving food on your plate. You must get it out of your mind that it's sinful to waste food, and realize that it's sinful to eat it if it's going to abuse your body. You may immediately learn to take the proper size helpings when you eat at home, but restaurant meals will *always* be in excess of what you should eat. Count on repeating "Leave a little—lose a little" throughout your lifetime when dining out.

In learning to use psychofusion, you have learned to use your mind to go to a feeling you choose for yourself. In effect, you are taking a "mind trip." You can invent more trips to help you with any specific eating problem you might have.

For instance, if you are irresistibly drawn to sugar, visualize a tombstone glistening in the sun. As you approach it, you can see it sparkle invitingly. When you get close to it, you realize the tombstone is made of sugar. That's what causes it to shine so brilliantly. But look closer at the tombstone. See the name on it. The name is yours. Sugar can kill you if you eat too much. It can write your name on a tombstone before your time.

Believe me, if your subconscious emotionalizes that idea about sugar, you will no longer be irresistibly drawn to eat it. I've had hundreds of clients tell me they see a tombstone every time they reach for a piece of candy. They cease reaching for it very often.

Another mind trip can be very effective in helping you eat less in a restaurant. Picture yourself sitting in a restaurant you enjoy. Visualize the decor and the dinner menu. Order your favorite dinner, and see yourself begin to eat it. Experience the taste in your mouth. Swallow and feel it go down your throat. Continue visualizing yourself eating these foods you enjoy until you have eaten just slightly more than half your meal.

Suddenly a person you admire comes to your table—someone you'd love to talk to. Maybe it's the president, or a book author, or a movie star you're fond of. This person is very cordial in his conversation with you, and you ignore your food while the two of you talk to each other. Experience this conversation until the person has to leave.

Feel happiness because this person bothered to be interested in you. After you tell him goodbye, you can continue eating your dinner if you feel like it. Once you get used to mentally leaving food on your plate after an imaginary experience in a restaurant, you will be able to leave real food uneaten in a real restaurant, especially if you supplement this mind trip with "Leave a little, lose a little."

To train yourself to turn down a dessert when you want it, but know you shouldn't have it, picture yourself sitting at your own kitchen table. See all the details—the placemats or tablecloth, the centerpiece, the plates, and especially the particular dessert you're craving. Feel yourself sitting in the chair. Are you comfortable? Settle back and relax.

Begin talking to the chair across the table from you. State one side of your conflict. Tell the chair why you would like to eat the dessert. Describe the particular ingredients that appeal to you. Then visualize yourself rising from the chair where you are sitting, walking half way around the table, and sitting down in the opposite chair. Explain the opposite side of the conflict. Estimate the number of calories the dessert has. Criticize the ingredients for their junk food qualities.

When you have finished, move again to the first chair and mentally continue the debate. Continue to change chairs and examine both sides of the question until you have reached a decision about having the dessert. Once you get used to talking yourself out of an imaginary dessert, you will be able to do this mental trip quickly when you're tempted with a real dessert.

To help you slow down your eating, picture yourself sitting at your own kitchen table with your family. Visualize each member of the family in detail. See the food on the table—whatever particular meal you care to imagine. See the platters and bowls being passed around the table. Watch the helpings everyone takes. See yourself taking helpings that are reasonable in size.

When you lift your fork to take the first bite, something strange happens. You notice that your movements are suddenly in slow motion. It takes much longer than usual to get your fork to your mouth, and it feels light and feathery in your hand. You feel very graceful and a sense of calmness spreads throughout your body. Enjoy the feeling. Enjoy the slow pace.

Look at the other members of your family. They seem to be shoveling down food as fast as they can get it to their mouths. They look like a movie scene playing at high speed. You feel amusement at how ridiculous they look as you continue to calmly, slowly finish your meal.

Everyone finishes before you, but you don't care. When you finish what's on your plate, you have no desire for a second helping. Once you get used to imagining slow motion eating, you will be able to slow down your eating at a real meal.

Don't scoff at imaginary mind trips until you try them. The subconscious doesn't care if the situation is real or imagined, and your subconscious controls your eating. Don't hesitate to try any of these methods to get the 90 percent of you that's emotional to agree with the 10 percent of you that intellectually wants to lose weight.

The subconscious likes symbolism, and mind trips supply it.

With these psychofusion and auto-echo techniques, you're doing all you can to help your subconscious make the attitude change that can lead to a body change. You're doing the best for your mind, so be sure to do the best for your body too.

Have a physical check-up to determine if your overweight has a physiological cause. The chances are slim, but if a physiological reason exists, follow your doctor's orders to correct the problem. Your general health is important. Unhealthy people gain weight because if a person feels bad, he usually eats to feel better.

Supplementing your weight loss plan with vitamins is wise. Give yourself all the breaks, and get on with your plans to dump the accidental conditioning program that's screwed up your emotional base. You're going to change that plugged-in script to enable yourself to have a mature, adult attitude about yourself. It isn't easy, but you can do it.

If you're a student, you make a commitment to go to class for a certain time period before you graduate. You dedicate yourself to doing what is required, you get grades as you go along, and when you finish, you get your credit.

Making a life change to accomplish a body change works on the same principle. Give yourself a schedule. Do the only thing that is required: eat less and enjoy life more. You'll have no need to impose penalities upon yourself, such as eating only in the same room, in the same chair, in the same clothes, from the same plate, with the same fork at the same time each day.

As you begin to lose weight, you will notice certain physical changes. You won't feel hungry like you used to. You'll find yourself eating slower, chewing your food longer. Before long you'll discover you no longer want to finish your regular food helpings. One day it'll occur to you that you no longer have an appetite between meals and that your craving for sweets has disappeared.

You'll find yourself accomplishing more because the time you formerly spent eating will be dedicated to something more constructive. You'll have more energy, and you'll find yourself exercising more without hating it.

Until you decided to make a life change, food was the positive stroke you had been giving yourself. Now all your changes deserve positive strokes, so tell yourself, "That's pretty neat," or "I like me pretty good," or "Dynamite, I'm going to be great." Stroke yourself. You deserve it.

You'll realize you no longer think about food. You no longer need it as an escape. You'll know you're maturing and abandoning the childhood programming that kept you from being the slim person you wanted to be.

Stick to your schedule. Nothing can keep you from graduating and receiving your credit. You can lose weight permanently and painlessly. You'll like yourself better, and your body will be the billboard of your mind. You will be a totally positive package of humanity—inside and out.

**INSTANT RECALL:** "Only a fat head lives in a fat body."

# CHAPTER 20

# Converting Yourself to a Non-Smoker

MOST SMOKERS TRY to kick the habit by simply giving up cigarettes. Repressing the urge to smoke 30, 40, or 50 times a day, they get irritable, feel deprived, and shout or cry a lot. That's why statistics show more than 80 percent of all people who try to stop smoking on their own fail. Eventually they succumb to the urge to continue sucking nicotine into their lungs.

Giving up cigarettes is not the way to stop smoking. The only permanent and comfortable way to stop smoking is to convert yourself to a non-smoker. If you can convert yourself to a non-smoker, you will not be giving up something you still want to do. You will stop smoking simply because you no longer have the urge to.

As a hypnotherapist, I have helped more than 15,000 smokers reprogram their emotional subconscious minds to become non-smokers. Although hypnotism is the quick way to reprogram parts of our subconscious minds that we do not like, reprogramming can be done on your own. You can convert yourself to a non-smoker with psychofusion and auto-echo.

First, admit to yourself that you really don't want to quit. Smokers like to smoke. The emotional part of your mind likes the feeling, the pleasure, and the gratification of smoking, even though the intellectual, logical part of your mind wants to quit. Smoking is a feel, not a think. That's why you often smoke and at the same time reprimand yourself for doing it. Your intelligence tells you smoking is dumb, but your emotions don't care.

You know when the 90 percent of you that's emotional starts arguing with the 10 percent of you that's intellectual, the emotions almost always win the debate. The rational part of your mind shouts, "Quit!" while the emotional part screams out for the physical and psychological lift of a cigarette. The emotional part says, "I don't care, I like it, I'm doing it." To convert yourself to a non-smoker, you must get the emotional part of your mind to agree with your intellectual desire to quit.

Your emotional satisfaction at being a non-smoker must be as strong as your emotional hook to be a smoker presently is. Only then can you be a person who is simply not interested in lighting up a cigarette, as opposed to somebody who quits smoking but still wants to light up every time he finishes a meal, has a cup of coffee, talks on the telephone, drives his car, or sips a cocktail.

First you need an emotionally charged reason for not smoking. You have to determine a gut feel for why you are quitting. You must know what the payoff will be.

If you smoke, there's a payoff right then, both physically and psychologically. The nicotine sucked into your body causes the liver to convert stored animal starch into sugar. The sugar is then released into the blood stream, giving you a metabolic boost comparable to eating a candy bar. A cigarette, which also deadens certain nerve endings, gives you a speedy, pleasant physical high, while satisfying your psychological need to experience the ritual of lighting the cigarette and the oral gratification of dragging that last bit of pleasure out of it.

Although the tar in cigarettes gives them their flavor, nicotine is the element that causes physical addiction. When that extra shot of sugar gives you the pleasant high, it also triggers a squirt of insulin from the pancreas, lowering the blood sugar level and bringing on a gradual feeling of fatigue or tension. The fatigue or tension leads to the desire for the high of another cigarette to overcome the bad feeling. You as a smoker know very well the constant cycle caused by cigarettes because of the immediate gratification smoking gives.

When you quit smoking, you're looking for long-term gratification. You know that two or three months from the time you quit, you're going to feel terrific. Your breathing will be easier, your sense of smell will be improved, and your taste buds will be more sensitive. But that doesn't help your situation now. It's *now* when you're bugged, wanting to light up that cigarette for gratification right this instant.

You've got that physical reality of your body screaming for more nicotine, and you've got that psychological hangup that keeps replaying the same tape in your subconscious, emotional mind: "Hey, where's my goodie that makes me feel better?" The stimulus for immediate gratification is strong because it's emotionally charged. You need an equally emotionally charged reason to quit smoking without painful withdrawal symptoms.

Ask yourself, if you become a non-smoker, what's the payoff? You need an eventual payoff worth forfeiting the immediate payoff of smoking. You need a payoff that tightens your stomach and makes your subconscious say, "Hey, that's good. That's worth it to me." You've got to convert your subconscious to agree with your conscious, intellectual mind and its decision to stop smoking. This conversion is vital because if the two are in conflict, the subconscious will win, and you'll go back to smoking.

If you think improving your health is a good enough reason for quitting, forget it. Smokers generally *think* they want to quit smoking for their health, but that's a joke. Notice, I said "think."

Health sounds like a good reason to give up cigarettes, but it isn't. If it were, people whose doctors have warned them to stop smoking would do so. They don't! They go back to the same doctor for their physical check-up year after year, and year after year they get the same advice which they don't heed. Health doesn't have the emotional hook needed to make your emotional mind want to stop smoking. There's no emotional hook because you aren't sick. You know you're damaging your body when you smoke, but there's no immediate pain.

If the doctor said, "You've damaged your larynx, and we're going to have to remove your voice box," that might be a health reason emotionally charged enough to convert you to a non-smoker. But health reasons won't cut it until they hit home. You know a two-pack-a-day smoker has a life expectancy eight to nine years shorter than a non-smoker the same age, but you're still kicking now. You know 90 percent of all lung cancer cases are smokers, and 90 percent of them die within five years, but your lungs are still breathing in and out easily enough. You know that each year 325,000 Americans die from causes traceable to smoking, but you don't care about facts. Facts don't matter until they hurt emotionally. Forget health as an emotionally charged reason to become a non-smoker.

A second reason smokers give for wanting to quit is to save money, but that reason won't work either. Remember the smokers who years ago swore they'd stop when cigarettes went up to 50 cents a pack? Even though they cost much more than that now, those same smokers are still in there puffing. Each year American smokers spend more than $8 billion on cigarettes, but a smoker doesn't resent his share of the tab.

Smokers are aloof to the fact that smoking costs more than just the average $450 a year spent by a two-pack person. Not only are there expenses involved in lighters, ashtrays, and holes burned in good clothes or carpets, there are hidden costs of more than $17 billion a year on health care costs and absenteeism due to smoking. Statistics show that smokers have more illnesses and more chronic diseases leading to early disability than non-smokers. They have more work absenteeism and more work accidents than non-smokers, along with twice as many auto accidents.

The 200,000 yearly fires traceable to smoking or matches used in smoking—more than 25 percent of all fires in the United States—cause some 2,000 deaths and result in $100 million in property losses. The hidden costs of smoking are so vast that 40 life insurance companies in the United States offer discount policy rates for non-smokers. But smokers don't mind paying the higher premiums. To give up the smoking habit, a smoker needs a much stronger reason than to save money.

A third reason smokers give for wanting to quit smoking is to please other members of their family. Some family member who is tired of inhaling second-hand smoke and living in a stale-smelling house is putting the pressure on the smoker to give up his nasty habit. The smoker is feeling guilty and frustrated, and any smoker can tell you what happens when he feels guilty and frustrated. He lights a cigarette. A smoker smokes more when under stress than at any other time. So forget quitting to please someone else. You can choose to become a non-smoker only for yourself, and only then if you find an emotionally charged reason to do it.

What type reason will work?

The ideal emotional charge would be traumatization, but that's hard to plan. Traumas just happen, but when they do, they give the gut feeling that will work when an intellectual, logical, informational, rational feeling won't. The best kind of emotional charge would tell your subconscious, "I've got to make a change. I've got no choice." If you don't have such a charge, you need to find one.

Don't bother throwing away your cigarettes and lighter until you've intellectually decided on the emotional charge strong enough for you. Only then will you be able to use psychofusion to integrate that intellectual reason into your subconscious mind so that it, too, wants to convert you to a non-smoker.

**INSTANT RECALL:** "Smoking is for suckers."

# CHAPTER 21

# Finding a Reason to Stop Smoking

YOU FEEL HOOKED on cigarettes. You feel they're your friend, your buddy, your pal. You must accept that they are not! You must depersonalize the cigarettes. They were here before you were born, and they'll be here when you're dead. They're just something that happened to you, like having an ugly wart on your nose. You have a choice about the wart. You can keep it and feel ugly, or you can have it removed and say, "I didn't want it, I didn't pick it, I'll get rid of it."

Do the same with cigarettes. Depersonalize them and accept the fact they're an emotional, accidental circumstance in your life. They're something you got into which made a pattern in your life, like being right- or left-handed. You didn't pick being right-handed either, but now it's a pattern for you. You've matured to the point that you can eliminate things you didn't choose, if you don't want them. Although there's no reason to eliminate being right-handed, there are plenty of reasons to eliminate cigarettes.

Don't feel guilty about your smoking habit. You didn't choose to be a smoker. You may have chosen to be accepted by your peers who were smoking like adults while you were still thinking like a kid. You may have chosen to mimic a movie star while you were trying to grow up. Some circumstantial environmental pressure made it necessary for you to learn to smoke, so you don't need to feel guilty about it. It's one of those accidents that happened to you because you were unlucky.

Try to develop an aversion for cigarettes because they are eating up your body, easily, gradually, and steadily. Every time you smoke a cigarette, your heart beat increases 40 percent or about 25 beats a minute. That's some 5,000 extra heart beats per pack. As soon as you light that cigarette up, your body begins to react to the attack of the poison. Your blood pressure immediately increases 10 to 20 points. The walls of your arteries constrict by an average of 22 percent.

When you smoke, you destroy 25 milligrams of Vitamin C for every cigarette. That lowers your resistance to infections, and the body system can't fight the minor infections and viruses. Smoking also destroys the B vitamins in your body. You cut the supply to the nerve endings in your body, and your body can't function in a normal way. When you inhale, the smoke is often as high as 190 degrees in temperature.

When you smoke, you're artificially stimulating your nervous system, causing your body to react in a way that's uncomfortable and leads to serious disease. When you smoke, you're inhaling 50 times more arsenic than is legally allowed in the same amount of food. You're paralyzing the mobile cleansing system of the respiratory tract so that your body cannot clean the air that goes into your body as it normally would be able to do.

When you smoke, funny little things happen. Your field of vision is cut by 22 percent due to the paralysis of the nerve endings in the eyeballs, but you don't notice that when you're smoking. Your body compensates; you become used to it. When you smoke, it puts an immediate strain on your liver, which is the poison filter of your body. It's overworked when you smoke.

When you smoke, you're promoting an addiction to a drug called nicotine, which your body cannot build a tolerance for. When you smoke, there's an increase in stomach acidity that irritates your stomach lining. Smoking dulls and deadens the taste buds in your mouth as the smoke trickles down through your throat and into your lungs. When you smoke, your blood sugar level rises rapidly, and then drops rapidly when you end the smoking.

Smoking cuts your oxygen supply to the brain by 50 percent and cuts your memory 10 to 23 percent. Smoking promotes wrinkles by lowering your skin temperature three to six degrees. It also has an adverse effect not only on the heart, blood vessels, and nervous system, but on the digestive tract and kidneys. When you inhale, more than 85 percent of the smoke's volatile chemicals and more than 50 percent of its carbon monoxide stay in your lungs. You subtract six minutes from your life with each cigarette you smoke.

Smokers account for 80 percent of all vocal

cord cancers in the United States and 90 percent of all lung cancer cases. Twice as many smokers as non-smokers have peptic ulcers. Women who both smoke and use oral contraceptives increase 10 times their risks of heart attacks. The more a pregnant woman smokes, the smaller her baby's length, chest size, and head size. A mother's smoking during pregnancy also increases by 52 percent a newborn's chance of dying from crib death syndrome.

Tobacco smoke contains seven known cancer-producing agents and 15 chemical substances known to be poisonous to human life. Cyanide, one chemical in smoke, is the gas previously used to execute criminals in gas chambers. Formaldehyde is used to embalm dead bodies, but smokers suck it into their bodies with every puff. Nicotine itself is an organic nerve drug so powerful that a one-drop injection would cause immediate death. If you ate three cigarettes, you'd be dead within thirty minutes because the nicotine would go directly into your blood stream and kill you. It would take only two of the strong kind like Camels or Lucky Strikes to do you in.

A smoker who smokes one pack of cigarettes a day for 15 years absorbs the equivalent of an 8-ounce cup of tar each year. The concentration of poisonous carbon monoxide in cigarette smoke is at least 1,000 times greater than the allowable environmental level. Once lighted, a cigarette contaminates the air for around 12 minutes. That's why parents who smoke contribute to impaired respiratory conditions in their children.

An estimated 53.3 million Americans smoke, and more than 300,000 smoke themselves to death each year. An estimated 6 million teenagers and at least 100,000 children under 13 smoke regularly. Each day an additional 4,000 American children try smoking for the first time.

Former Secretary of Health, Education and Welfare Joseph A. Califano Jr. declared smoking to be the nation's number one health problem, saying "Today there can be no doubt that smoking is truly slow-motion suicide." Overwhelming evidence supports his contention.

Smokers know cigarettes are not good for them. Many feel they must be stupid because they smoke when they know how unhealthful cigarettes are. They feel their smoking habit is a direct assault upon their intelligence, but that's ridiculous. Sigmund Freud died of jaw and mouth cancer, and even after he knew he had the disease, he still chewed on his cigars. Many of the world's geniuses have been smokers.

You associate smoking with "feeling" things such as finishing a meal, following sex, awakening in the morning, watching television, drinking alcohol or coffee, talking on the phone. When you convert yourself to a non-smoker, you will enjoy these activities for their own emotional gratification, not because they signal a cigarette.

Be honest with yourself about using cigarettes to help you relieve anxiety, repress anger, contain your appetite, escape unpleasant realities, and express either manliness or feminine sophistication. Knowing why you smoke will help you develop mature methods to fill these emotional needs.

When I help a person stop smoking with hypnosis, I often regress him to his first cigarette. Consciously you might not remember your first cigarette, but your subconscious never forgets. Your subconscious can tell you the friends you were with, the brand cigarette you tried, and the description of the place where the big event took place.

The subconscious remembers how you had to suffer while learning to smoke. You had to practice diligently to get past the coughing stage and to accustom your taste buds to the nasty, biting taste. When I regress a subject to his first cigarette, he sucks the imaginary smoke into his lungs and coughs. He tries to spit out the terrible taste. When I ask him why he is doing this to his body, his answer is almost always the same: "All my friends smoke." Usually, he's 15, 16 or 17 years old when he decides to join the gang.

It's a rare bird who starts smoking when he's 25 years old. Smokers are like fingernail biters, or bedwetters or stutterers—nobody starts doing those things when they're in their twenties. The accident that forces you to cigarettes either gets you when you're young, or not at all. Smoking is a childhood or teenage pattern that's picked up and carried into an adult level. Recognizing it as an age-regressive type of behavior might give you the emotional charge you need to eliminate it from your life.

Think of other things you used to do when you were that age: cruising down Main Street trying to pick someone up, spending half whatever salary or allowance you had on records, spending half your life listening to them, getting out of work whenever you could, staying in bed until Mom pulled you out. When you think of those other things you did when you were 15 years old, you realize you couldn't make it in the adult world if you had continued all those habits until you were 37. But you continued smoking.

Start to think of smoking as a throwback to your teenage years that no longer fits, now that you're an adult. Just as teeth grinders and knuckle crackers are holding onto childhood habits accidentally programmed into them before they reached emotional maturity, so are you as a smoker. Smoking isn't appropriate for you as an adult. To eliminate it, you need emotional reprogramming that leads to ego maturation. You will get it when you choose to reprogram yourself as a non-smoker with psychofusion. You will mature the part of you that keeps you hooked to a childhood pattern.

You'll recognize cigarettes for what they really are: an adult pacifier. You were born sucking for air and sucking for food to satisfy your inborn oral gratification needs. You learn quickly that your mouth is a pretty important thing, and sticking something in it continues to fulfill physical and emotional needs throughout life. Nail biters, munchie crunchers, gum and toothpick chewers all have their own kind of emotional crutch, but their oral gratification habit won't kill them like cigarettes will kill you. I don't know of anybody who ever died from biting his fingernails, but cigarettes *will* kill you. The question is not *if*, but when. It's just a question of time.

You must find a reason strong enough to make you quit. If you had a parent or a close relative who died of emphysema, or a heart attack, or another problem related to cigarettes, you might be able to plug an emotionally charged health reason into your subconscious. You're a piece of that person because you came from him genetically. You can honestly tell yourself that your chances of ending up the same way are extremely high. If you can picture that person, get the feeling of his suffering, relive it like it's your own, and plug it into yourself, you may have found the payoff that will work to convert you to a non-smoker.

An aversion to the dirtiness of smoking can sometimes be an incentive strong enough to charge a person to quit. Look at the holes in your clothes. Do you think your boss doesn't notice the hole you burned in the lapel of your $350 navy blue suit the first day you wore it? Do you think passengers in your compact car aren't repulsed by the stale smell emanating from your air conditioner?

Look at the ashes that didn't quite make your living room ashtray—those scattered around the walnut table top and those ground into the shag carpet. Do you like being such a slob? Cup your hands around your mouth, blow, and smell your breath. It's crummy, you know. That's the way you smell to other people.

If you can get an aversion to the filthiness of smoking, it might become an emotional charge strong enough to convert you to a non-smoker. Your payoff will be to eliminate an offensive element in your life and become a more socially acceptable person.

Anger is an emotion strong enough to make you quit—if you can let yourself get angry enough about your smoking habit. Get furious at the way tobacco companies seduce you to make you want to smoke. Look at the ads with the beautiful girls seductively holding cigarettes in their fingertips, phallic symbols directed to your subconscious mind. Get furious that tobacco companies are subliminally selling sex every time they hustle you to smoke, picturing macho men with mustaches and tattoos. When they manipulate you with their ads, they don't advertise smoking the way it really is. An honest ad would show a person with a ring through his nose, being jerked around by a cigarette all day. If you can get angry at the fact that cigarettes control your life that way, your anger might get your subconscious, emotional mind to agree with your intellectual desire to stop smoking.

One of my clients couldn't stop smoking until she found exactly the emotional charge that worked for her. An avid gardener, Jill missed smelling the roses and geraniums as she lovingly cared for them. Smoking had all but destroyed her sense of smell. Not only did she miss pleasant smells such as fresh bread baking in her kitchen and lemon oil on the furniture on cleaning day, she worried about unpleasant smells. How could she tell if her deodorant really worked? How could she tell if the storage closet was musty? The desire to smell was strong enough reason to work for this particular person.

You must find the reason strong enough for you, and repeat it to yourself mentally 10 or 20 times a day. It can't be a "think" reason; it must be a "feel." Just as Jill told herself over and over, "I am going to smell again," tell yourself over and over what your payoff is going to be.

Only then will you have your subconscious mind cooperating in your desire to be a nonsmoker.

**INSTANT RECALL:** "Quitting can't kill, but smoking will."

# CHAPTER 22

# Throwing Away
# Your Cigarettes

OKAY, YOU'RE READY to dump the cigarettes now. You recognize that you are not giving up something you want. Instead, you are converting yourself to something you want to be—a non-smoker.

You know you can do it because you've done it before. At some point in your life, you were a non-smoker before that unlucky accident that you didn't choose caused you to become a smoker. Look back at that point in your life—that point when you didn't smoke. It doesn't matter if you have to go back to when you were 16, 12, or 7—at whatever age you got hooked to the cigarette habit. If you can't remember when you first started smoking, look back to the time you had bronchitis and were unable to smoke until your lungs cleared. Or look back to the first months of your pregnancy when morning sickness turned you against cigarettes.

Go back in your memory to a time when you were a non-smoker. Get inside the memory, and let the feelings flood into your mind and body. The urge for a cigarette doesn't exist in that memory. Visualize yourself as you were then. Relive the moment. Remember your feelings. No nicotine in your system led to tension in those days. In those days you needed no emotional pacification from the ritual of reaching for a cigarette, lighting up, sucking on it, holding it, and using it as part of your social image. You liked yourself then, when you weren't a slave to a filthy, unhealthy habit. You smelled better, and food tasted better then—do you remember? Let the happy thoughts of that memory permeate your mind. See yourself and remember yourself as a non-smoker each time you mentally repeat your payoff for becoming a non-smoker.

There's only one right way to make the conversion you desire. Quit cold turkey. Forget the gradual cutting down. You must make a commitment either to quit or not to quit. It's much tougher to try to wean yourself gradually off cigarettes than to commit to smoking zero.

I've helped thousands of smokers become non-smokers with the help of hypnosis, but I've had only one client who was able to limit the number of cigarettes she smoked and continue smoking daily. At age 68, Verna still smoked three packs of cigarettes a day, and in spite of lung problems, she simply couldn't stop. After hypnotic suggestions didn't help her, we went to her subconscious to find out what would. The subconscious creates the problem, so it always knows the answer. Under hypnosis, Verna said she'd like to be able to smoke after her meals, the way she always did with her husband before he died. She wondered if cigarettes after her meals would give her the same comfort she used to have then, when she and her husband enjoyed those quiet moments together.

"Would it be acceptable for you to smoke only three cigarettes a day for the rest of your life?" I asked her. "Three cigarettes won't kill you like three packs a day will do. Would those supply enough emotional satisfaction to cover you the whole day?"

Verna decided they would. She was unable to give up cigarettes completely. She had lost her husband, and if she lost her cigarettes, she'd feel she had zip—nothing. Although her conscious mind had told me she wanted to stop smoking completely, her subconscious mind knew better. Her subconscious knew that three cigarettes at appropriate times during a day could give her the gratification she needed with the 48 years of marriage they symbolized.

For most people, it's better to give up cigarettes completely because total commitment is easier than controlled maintenance. But limiting cigarettes worked for Verna. A year later she was still smoking her three cigarettes a day and feeling terrific. Her lungs had cleared up, and she was all set to enjoy the later years of her life.

Verna was an exception. Perhaps one smoker in 100,000 could limit cigarettes the way she did. If you like those odds, good luck. I'll put my money on the smoker who decides to go cold turkey.

If you are to be comfortable as a non-smoker,

the things that made you smoke must begin to reverse themselves for you. Concentrate on reversing the stimulus-response conditioning that has caused you to light up. When you see someone else smoke, have a positive reaction. Feel good that you no longer have to suck that poison into your body. Tell yourself that the smoker has no choice. He has to smoke, but you don't.

Such a positive reaction will take practice on your part. Most people react negatively, with their tongues hanging out, wishing they too could light up. They think "They have one, I don't have one, I want one, I'm going to get one." You have to reprogram that language to, "They have to have one. Smokers have to smoke, but I don't. They look like fools over there sucking on that thing like a little kid, and I don't have to do that."

Begin observing the negative elements of smoking. Watch how people fool around with a cigarette like it's a toy. Watch how they suck on it like their lives depended upon it. Watch how smoking seems the biggest event in a smoker's life. Smoking will begin to look dumb to you. It will seem ridiculous. You will eventually begin to tell yourself, "I don't want to look like that. I want to mature beyond that stage." You will begin to feel the pride of being a non-smoker.

When tension or anxiety makes you crave a cigarette, rub your thumb and forefinger together four or five times. This physical trade-off will give you something to think about until the craving for a cigarette passes. What's more, it will satisfy your subconscious. Your subconscious mind really doesn't care what happens to relieve anxiety, but it will need an adequate substitute for the cigarettes it's been getting. It'll be just as happy for the anxiety or tension to be relieved in an area that doesn't matter to anybody. Other people care when you blow smoke in their eyes. Nobody cares about your rubbing your thumb and forefinger together—not even your subconscious.

When you were a smoker, you got a feeling of euphoria when the nicotine deadened the nerve endings and increased the blood sugar level. You can get that same feeling to some degree with deep breathing. Taking a deep breath floods your body with oxygen and just plain makes you feel good. When you convert to being a non-smoker, you'll enjoy inhaling air instead of hot, biting smoke.

Walking a half mile a day will help you convert to a non-smoker. While walking, practice deep breathing and accomplish two purposes at one time. Walking briskly enough to work up a mild perspiration helps eliminate the cigarette's poison residues from your body quicker. Drinking water several times a day will also help to flush these toxic elements from your body quicker.

The first few days might be difficult because of your physical withdrawal from the nicotine, but within three to five days nicotine will be totally gone from your body—if you're a normal person with a decent metabolism. After that, there's no physical addiction, but your psychological addiction can cause you to crave cigarettes for months or years unless you successfully psych yourself to become a non-smoker. It takes a maximum of two years for your body to completely cleanse itself of cigarette's effects. Even if you're 112 years old and seldom move a muscle, your blood vessels will clean themselves out, and your lungs will turn back to pink within two years.

If you miss the oral gratification of sucking on a cigarette, substitute something in its place when you first quit smoking. Many people chew on a toothpick, while others actually dangle a cigarette holder from their mouths. Such substitutes are usually easily discarded five or six days after becoming a non-smoker. A good oral gratification substitute is Vitamin C tablets, which you can chew several times a day. Cigarettes have been robbing your body of Vitamin C, which you can replenish while also satisfying your oral needs. Brushing your teeth several times a day will also help fill your oral need while giving you the added benefit of having a clean tasting mouth. After becoming accustomed to a non-smoker's clean tasting mouth, you won't want a smoker's rotten mouth any more.

Satisfy the manual need you had for cigarettes. Put an empty pack of cigarettes in your pocket or your purse—wherever you carried your cigarettes. When you automatically reach for them, you'll find something there to eliminate any possible feeling of deprivation. The empty pack not only gives you the security that something is there, it also reminds you that you're a non-smoker now. Carry that empty pack until you find that you no longer automatically reach for it.

Get rid of all the ashtrays, cigarettes, and lighters in your house. Play the out-of-sight and out-of-mind game. If you find yourself craving a cigarette while driving, don't hesitate to remove your car ash tray and store it in the glove compartment for a while.

Start stroking yourself for your decision to be a

non-smoker. Tell yourself you're being special, you're being mature, and you're making an advancement in your life. Tell yourself you are not giving up anything. Instead you are choosing to be something you've already been at one time in your life. Instead of feeling deprived, as people do who give up smoking simply by repressing the desire to smoke, you should feel proud of your decision to be a non-smoker.

Repeat your payoff mentally several times a day. Let your mind drift back to a memory of yourself as a non-smoker. Pull that memory out of your subconscious, like pulling a file out of a filing cabinet, and drift back to it. Visualize it. Keep the positive motivators of your payoff and your psychofusion working for you.

Most people who are serious in their desire to stop smoking can succeed with these positive motivators. Others need negative motivators to help them, like a direct assault on the ego.

Have a friend or relative who wants you to stop smoking take a convict-style, sideview picture of you with a cigarette hanging out of your mouth, unsupported by your hands. Then have him take another picture of you without the cigarette. Put both pictures side by side in a place where you'll see them frequently every day. Each time you look at the pictures, ask yourself which view you'd like to present to the public.

Make a large bet with someone that you'll quit smoking for a certain period of time, such as three months. Be sure the amount is large enough to scare you, but small enough to be reasonable. A $500 bill should do it. If you start craving a cigarette, the idea of paying $500 for the privilege will turn you right off to lighting up. You must, however, make this bet with somebody who will stick to the bargain and insist on collecting. It'll never work if you know the person is going to pat you on the head and say, "That's okay. You can keep the money." Clarify collecting procedures when you make the bet.

For another negative motivator, use the psycho-fusion technique to regress to a negative memory. Drift back and visualize yourself smoking your first cigarette. See yourself as you cough and sputter, trying to impress somebody else. Get inside the feeling you had then when you were trying to belong and be acceptable to your peers. Take that feeling and mature it. Say, "I'm not a kid anymore, I don't have to smoke to impress people."

If you can't remember your first cigarette, visualize a bad smoking memory, such as a time when you tried a Camel and almost choked, or a time when you were very ill and got even sicker when you smoked. Take those feelings and tell yourself you don't want to repeat them. Negative reinforcement may help you through the rough period of becoming a non-smoker.

Using other visual images with psychofusion has helped many of my clients through the first bad days of stopping their smoking habits. Visualize a cigarette on a blackboard. Then see yourself slowly erasing the cigarette with the corner of a blackboard eraser. Tell yourself, "I'm erasing the cigarette from the board, from my mind, and from my life."

Another technique involves emotionally accepting that if you eat three cigarettes, you'll be dead in 30 minutes. The fact is true. Close your eyes and see yourself chewing up three cigarettes. Imagine the feeling of holding something in your mouth that you know will kill you if you swallow. Get inside the feeling of aversion, and make a decision whether to swallow the cigarettes and die, or to spit them out of your mouth and live. See yourself physically spitting them out as you say to yourself, "I'm spitting them out of my mouth, out of my mind, and out of my life."

Both of the above psychofusion techniques might seem ridiculous to your intellectual conscious mind, but they are meaningful to your emotional subconscious mind. The subconscious likes symbolism, and these psychofusion techniques supply symbolic aversion to help change your subconscious attitude toward smoking.

Another emotional charge that will turn your subconscious off to cigarettes is to visualize a child you love, at his present age, smoking a cigarette. When you see a sweet, innocent 10-year-old with a cigarette dangling from his mouth and smoke curling up causing his eyes to water, your subconscious won't like that scene. It'll be turned right off and will help you turn off any lingering urge to light up.

Bring back any negative memory of cigarettes that you can remember. Flash back to the time you burned a hole in your new cashmere sweater, or the time you dropped a cigarette in a glass of water and were repulsed when that ugly brown stream started running down the water. Retrieve these memories because they are realities. If someone tells you you're going to die if you don't stop smoking, that's not a reality to your subconscious. You haven't died yet, but you have had negative experiences with smoking.

Take a deep breath and let it physically flood your body and your brain with oxygen. Exhale slowly, and say, "melt and relax." Visualize yourself having no desire to smoke even when others around you are puffing away. Train your subconscious to say, "I'm proud to be a nonsmoker" every time a smoker lights a cigarette. When this thought pattern becomes automatic to you, you'll get a visual stroke every time a smoker gives in to the habit that you have managed to overcome.

Remember, you are not suppressing the urge to smoke. That won't work in the long run. You are creating a non-smoker on the subconscious level. You've got to get your subconscious to accept the fact that you're a non-smoker, as opposed to somebody who can't smoke but still wants to.

You can do it. You can choose to be what you want to be instead of accepting the way you turned out by accident. The idea of smoking will begin to die in your mind. By your own choice, you will begin to think and feel and live—permanently and positively—like a non-smoker.

**INSTANT RECALL:** "Stop smoking and light up on my own."

# PART FOUR

# Choosing a
# Choice Life

# CHAPTER 23

# Rejecting Life's Adverse Accidents

PEOPLE TAKE THEIR feelings too seriously and too personally, especially negative feelings. They would rather feel joy than anger, confidence than fear, competence than ineptness, love than hate, pride than guilt. But they accept the first automatic feeling the subconscious mind spouts out, and they dismally believe, "That's just me. That's the way I am."

You know now that you don't have to settle for accidental feelings programmed into your subconscious, and you know how to use your mind's components cooperatively to select feelings you'd prefer. Because you have every possible human emotion within you, you can choose the best to make yourself a better person.

Take a look at the choices you've made so far. Your life was an accident from Day-One because you didn't choose to be born. At least 78 million sperm cells were released in that historic ejaculation, but only one got home to produce you. If given the choice, you most probably would not have picked the sperm that started your accidental life.

Just as you didn't choose to live, you won't choose to die, but you will. In relation to all measured time, your life span represents less than the time it takes to flick a flashlight on and off, only temporarily illuminating the darkness. That's all the more reason it should be the life you want, not just the one you got stuck with by accident.

You didn't pick your parents, and we know they didn't pick you, so you don't need to take the responsibility for them or their feelings. If you've got a couple of losers for parents, that's tough rocks. If you keep trying to love them, feeling guilty and guiltier because the loving gets harder and harder, does your guilt change anything? Bury it. Your heritage is ancient history. Don't choose to punish yourself because of accidental parentage you wouldn't have chosen if given the chance.

You didn't pick your sex, you didn't pick your color, you didn't pick your nationality. You didn't pick your IQ, your height, your shoe size, the space between your eyes, or your tendency to have good or bad breath. If you came out with a combination you're pleased with, consider it a kiss from the creator.

You didn't choose your name, just as I didn't. How would you like to be a hypnotist with a name like mine: James Hoke, as in "hocus pocus," or as frequently mispronounced, hokey? The descendants of Dr. Mudd, who treated the fleeing John Wilkes Booth, certainly learned what it's like for a "name to be mud." Still, most people—other than Hollywood hopefuls—stick with their monikers, miserable or not.

Would John Wayne have become famous as Marion Michael Morrison? Could Rock Hudson have made it as Roy Scherer or Kirk Douglas as Issur Danielovitch Demsky? Obviously, they had some doubts.

When you were five years old, did your parents give you a list of churches and ask you which one you wanted to attend? Of course, they didn't. You went where they went. You don't have a 5-year-old Baptist kid in a Catholic family or a 5-year-old Morman clamoring to convert to Judaism.

Just as you didn't pick your church, you didn't pick the guilt programmed in your subconscious when you started confessing your sins to some unseen guy in a booth before you could even differentiate mortal from venial or right from wrong. You didn't choose the confusion of an incomprehensible Latin church service and calling someone "Father" who wasn't your father and someone "Sister" who wasn't your sister.

Or you didn't choose not to celebrate Christmas every year when your neighbor buddies looked forward to Santa's delivering toys. You didn't choose to wear a funny little hat in the synogogue or to become a man at age 13 or never to eat bacon in your parents' home.

When you were a child, did your parents let you choose which words you'd like to be dirty and which you'd like to be clean? No, the dirty ones were the ones that made Mom angry, the ones you got spanked for saying. Some were words that kept you wondering and worrying because you were afraid to ask what they meant, let alone ask why adults could say them and you couldn't.

You didn't choose for "smooth" to be a good word and "snot" to be a bad word, for "son of a bitch" to be an insult, and "stud" to be a compliment. You didn't even choose your philosophical acceptance of a playboy sowing his wild oats, as opposed to your disapproval of a tramp who lays around.

Did you choose your elementary school—or simply attend the one designated by your school board? How about your high school and even your college? Were you qualified to pick the right college or able to afford it if you could? No, you probably chose a college a friend said was easy and a great party school. Or perhaps one far enough from home to foster your new-found freedom—or close enough to home to cling to mama, papa, and your security blanket.

Did you consciously and deliberately choose your husband or your wife? Did you place "spouse wanted" ads in Florida, Washington, Arizona, New York? Did you deliberately ferret out one prospective spouse after another to find the one exactly right for you? Most people didn't. Most people settled for the one who lived nearby, handy and available, the one who found them without extensive searching either.

If you're fat, you didn't choose your fat body. If one of your parents is fat, you had four chances out of 10 of also overtipping the scales. If both parents are fat, your odds were eight out of 10. That's not only hereditary but because you learn by following your parents' patterns. Girls wear their mothers' lipsticks and totter around in their high-heeled shoes. Boys hammer around the basement workshop and practice shaving in front of the mirror. Both sexes shovel food down their faces if the parents they love do the same.

If you smoke, you already know you didn't choose to be a smoker. You didn't consciously choose to struggle with a terrible-tasting cigarette until your body adapted to a nicotine addiction. No, but you probably chose to be accepted by your peers who were dragging on cigarettes, acting like adults, while you were standing around with your mouth gaping and your hands empty, just being a kid.

You also didn't choose your mother's gene that made you bald by age 32. You didn't choose your freckles or your hillbilly, Hoosier, or Harvard accent. Most people honestly didn't even choose their jobs. They were chosen for them by the qualifications they amassed while attending high schools and colleges they also didn't choose.

When you analyze the choices you've actually consciously made, the first feeling to pop from your subconscious might be anger—either anger at yourself for allowing your life to result from accidents, or anger at me for pointing out the things you didn't choose.

But you know you don't have to accept the first emotion that your subconscious pumps out. Using the psychofusion technique, step outside your emotion and observe it objectively.

Is there logic in being angry at yourself? Of course not. Whatever you've done with your life, you did the best you could do at the time.

Is there logic in being angry at me? Not if you accept my analysis of your choices in the manner in which it is intended—to turn you on to turning your life into what you choose on purpose, instead of what you ended up with accidentally.

Reject your anger, and replace it with hope. If you once felt no hope existed to help change your life the way you'd like it to be, you know better now. You know the key to change is there in your subconscious, waiting to help you turn on a better life.

Even if most of your life up to now has been accidental, the rest doesn't have to be. You can choose to change if you dislike the person your accidents created. You can tap your hidden capabilities to become the person you'd like to be.

**INSTANT RECALL:** "The ultimate choice is *always* mine."

# CHAPTER 24

# Being Your Best

AT AGE 85, Wilson purchased a brand new white Cadillac, as he had done every decade since he could first afford the luxury car. Upon getting it home, he made a decision to buy a different color after the next decade. He was afraid he was getting in a rut.

How many people at age 85 would face the ten years ahead with such optimism? Without knowing it, Wilson practiced psychofusion throughout his lifetime. He recognized he had a choice of how to feel about any situation—the choice of being optimistic or being pessimistic. If you learn to perpetuate the idea of being optimistic, as Wilson did, optimism can become a piece of your personality.

Because Wilson expects to live to age 95, his chances of doing so are greatly increased—any doctor will tell you that. If he had decided that his new white Cadillac would be his last, it probably would be.

Only you are in control of your destiny. Your family, your friends, your employer, your neighbors—they affect you only as much as you choose to let them. If you're allowing them to influence your life in a way you don't like, you're setting yourself up for certain kinds of accidents that perpetuate your accidental life.

Analyze the direction the accidents of your life are taking you. Recognize that the accidental evolution taking place in your life is only happening because you, yourself, let it happen. If you examine your accidents, you'll realize that they point out certain strengths and weaknesses in your personality. You're not perfect. Nobody is. But if you learn to recognize your weaknesses, you can intellectually decide how to overcome them and train your emotions to cooperate in any transformation you want to make.

Start by choosing the best way to look at any situation, and you will become a happier person. Your glass is either half full or half empty, depending upon the way you view it. An overcooked roast is either burned or nice and crispy. An old model, rusted-out car is either a junk heap or good transportation. An extremely small room is either crowded or cozy. You have the choice.

If you were an employer, which job candidate would you choose: the one who said, "It sounds like a lot of very hard work," or the one who said, "It sounds like a terrific challenge?"

In any situation you have two judgments, an intellectual one and an emotional one—what you

think about something and how you feel about it.
Until you learn to use the two parts of your mind
together, what you think about something will
strictly be a spin-off of how you feel about it.
When your subconscious automatically spouts out
a feeling, you must learn to intellectually tell yourself, "Wait a minute. I have a choice. I can change
that feeling if I want to."

Instead, most people pin themselves in with adverse self-fulfilling prophesies and accept their
negatives without challenge. If a man whose
father died a month after retirement spends the
last 20 years of his working life expecting to do the
same, he probably will. He accepts a pessimistic
choice rather than rejecting it for an optimistic attitude toward retirement.

A father tells his daughter that math will probably be her hardest subject, just as it was for him.
If she accepts that pessimistic prophesy, she'll certainly fulfill it. Let's face it—if she loves her
father and desires to emulate him in any way, her
subconscious will accept the prophesy without
question. How many 6-year-old kids can handle
the mental process of consciously making an optimistic choice? Children get programmed with
negative expectations that can haunt them
throughout their lives. The lucky get programmed
positively.

Greg was afflicted with an ugly birthmark on
his right cheek. Born in an era when cosmetic
surgery was a luxury reserved only for the rich, he
was destined to spend his growing years as an
unattractive young man. However, the birthmark
didn't bother Greg. He was active in high school
sports, was elected president of his senior class,

went on to excel in college, and made important contributions to mankind's progress in his profession as a scientist.

Why was Greg's life so positive, even though he was marked in a negative manner? Because his parents, devout Christians whose faith he shared, assured him from early childhood that God had marked him because he was destined to achieve special things. He lived his self-fulfilling prophesy, and luckily, it was a positive plug-in. Had the parents been embarrassed or ashamed by his ugly birthmark, Greg could just as easily have been a loser, rather than a winner.

Whatever negative choices, negative prophesies, and negative programming have been burrowed in your subconscious can be counteracted if you choose to make them positive. There is nothing in life that does not have some positive aspects, if you only choose to find them. The old adage, "Every cloud has a silver lining," can be true for you, if you practice finding the emotion that sifts the good from the bad and gives you positive feelings. Intellectually look for the good, find it, and with psychofusion, bring back the good feeling to go with it.

If you fall down the stairs and break your right leg, your first thought could be, "Terrific! I broke only one leg. That's great. I'll have a chance to catch up on my reading now. I'll get more done at the office—things I've been putting off doing—because it'll be too difficult to leave the office for other things. I may have one broken leg, but it gives me an opportunity to succeed at some things I've been putting off."

If your third-grade son is confined home with

chicken pox for two weeks, your first thought ought to be, "Great! We haven't had a chance for around-the-clock togetherness since Johnny started school. I'm going to have an opportunity to get to know Johnny better and to understand what he does at school because we'll have to keep up on his homework. We can have some fun times while he's home, playing checkers or baking chocolate chip cookies together. A parent would seldom have an opportunity for two weeks of closeness with a child, and I'm not going to let anything interfere with my enjoying his sickness."

If you wake up with a hangover, the good thing is—you woke up. If you suffer with bad breath, the good thing is—you're breathing. If you walk with a limp because of a birth deformity, the good things is—you walk.

When Maria's husband was sentenced to three years in jail, she looked at the good side of the misfortune. Because she had to get a job to support her two children and herself, she would become more independent while he was behind bars. His getting nailed for breaking the law made her want to become strong and supportive while he was gone, so that when he came back he would have something valuable to come back to and realize that he, too, could make it in life legally.

His conviction was actually lucky in some ways: the judge could have sentenced him to seven years, but he chose three instead. Being in jail for a minor crime might teach him the lesson he needed to prevent him from committing more serious crimes. The conviction could be the best thing that ever happened to him.

Maria is making it okay. When her husband is

released, she'll be a good wife for him if he, too, starts tackling life positively. If he goes back to his old ways, she'll be in a position to ditch him rather than let him pull her back to a negative life.

Positive thinking people are life's winners, and they don't let negative people pull them down. If a negative person becomes involved with a group of successful achievers, one of two things happens: either he becomes positive and rises to their level, or the achievers will eliminate him from their group. Achievers recognize that one rotten apple spoils the whole barrel. They subconsciously realize that if they allow a loser to stay, he'll gradually pull them down. So out he goes. You can push out your negative emotions the same way.

Attitudes are contagious. If you work around people who swear consistently, you'll eventually swear. If you move from the north to Georgia, you'll pick up a southern accent. If your friends are losers, they'll pull you down to their level. Likewise if you begin making every first thought a positive one, you'll become a positive thinker. Intellectually decide to expose yourself to positive feelings and your emotions will catch the mood you want. That's the way to psych yourself to success.

Carl became a successful insurance salesman because he approached all prospects positively. He told himself that no prospective customer was ever going to meet a more honest, involved, straight salesman than he. He enters every sales situation feeling that his product is superior and knowing that he's so honest in presenting it that customers should recognize those facts and buy from him. If they don't buy, it isn't his failure. It's because they couldn't recognize his sincerity and value to them, and he can't help that. That's their problem.

Luke became a winning wrestler because he psyched himself never to get pinned to the mat. He identified his body with television's Hulk, who gets a supersurge of strength that causes his clothes to pop off as his body expands. In a match, whenever Luke's back gets near the mat, he visualizes the Hulk and immediately gets a sudden surge of energy and power. With psychofusion, he uses a vision of the Hulk to get inside the feeling he needs to throw off his opponent.

Decide on a visual image to pop into your head everytime your subconscious gives you an emotion you don't want. If you're often depressed, find a memory of an extremely happy time. If you're worried, find a memory of carefree times. If you're often nervous, find a memory of a time when you were exceptionally calm. If those memories don't exist for you, you know what to do. Go out and get them. Create new memories with new experiences to give you what you need.

Ramble through your memories until you conjure up the details of your past that contain the feelings you want. Remember the specific colors, sounds, words—whatever gave you the feeling you found so desirable.

When you use psychofusion, it is vital to have several specific memories that you can visualize quickly and easily. You must train yourself to retrieve the memories from your subconscious with push-button speed and ease. Because your subconscious acts spontaneously in pushing unwanted emotions to the conscious level, you must learn to counteract them just as spontaneously.

You must use whatever memories you've selected over and over until they become a new part of your subconscious. "Melt and relax" will become your cue words to bring out the feelings you want. A deep inhale and exhale will become the vehicles through which your chosen emotions surface. Eventually, you will either mature or reject programmed feelings that conflict with your pleasant memories' feelings.

Psychofusion will work! You have the magic in your mind to make it work, as everyone does. As a hypnotist, I've seen the magic with thousands of clients who've stopped smoking, lost weight, overcame insomnia and impotence, conquered hypertension and fears, relieved menstrual and childbirth pains, improved study and recall skills, given up stuttering and nail biting, and developed positive self images. Psychofusion can work for whatever change you'd like to make.

You don't need a hypnotist to help you change. A hypnotist is like a coach. He knows what to do to win the game, but he can't do it himself. He can only teach his subject what to do. Because all hypnosis is self hypnosis, the hypnotist simply leads his subject to learn to resolve his own problems. He can give the subject the tools to accomplish changes in his behavior, but he can't make him willing.

If you're willing to use psychofusion to reprogram yourself for a better life, you can do it. All psychs are self-psychs. Like a coach, I've tried to turn you on to the way to score your touchdown, but I can't score it for you. You're the one carry-

ing the ball and doing the running, but now you
know you have a choice about the game plan. You
know how to fuse your intellect and emotions to
turn yourself on to the life that eluded you when
your subconscious and conscious minds were in
conflict.

You have the choice. You can make yourself a
winner if you don't let negative programming
tackle you before you've crossed the goal line.

**INSTANT RECALL:** "I'll be the best me I'm able
to be."

# If they can do it,
## so can you.

### But first find out *how* they did it.

Develop your success potential with these books written by and about people who have discovered the secret of getting ahead. If you want more out of life, these books are for you!

| | | |
|---|---|---|
| ___10000-6 | **THE WINNER'S EDGE**<br>Dr. Denis Waitley | $3.50 |
| ___07274-6 | **WITH NO FEAR OF FAILURE**<br>Thomas J. Fatjo, Jr. and Keith Miller | $2.95 |
| ___08530-9 | **THE DOUBLE WIN**<br>Dr. Denis Waitley | $3.95 |
| ___07456-0 | **BELIEVE!**<br>Richard M. Devos with Charles Paul Conn | $2.95 |
| ___10170-3 | **THE ULTIMATE SECRETS OF TOTAL SELF CONFIDENCE**<br>Dr. Robert Anthony | $3.50 |
| ___09354-9 | **THE ART OF THINKING**<br>Allen F. Harrison and Robert Bramson, M.D. | $3.50 |
| ___10067-7 | **I WOULD IF I COULD AND I CAN**<br>James H. Hoke | $3.50 |